Mountain Biking
Chico

MARK M. MENARD

FALCON® Helena, Montana

A FALCON GUIDE®

Falcon® Publishing is continually expanding its list of recreation guidebooks. All books include detailed descriptions, accurate maps, and all the information necessary for enjoyable trips. You can order extra copies of this book and get information and prices for other Falcon® guidebooks by writing Falcon, P.O. Box 1718, Helena, MT 59624 or calling toll free 1-800-582-2665. Also, please ask for a free copy of our current catalog.
Visit our website at www.FalconOutdoors.com

©1999 by Falcon® Publishing, Inc., Helena, Montana

Printed in Canada

1 2 3 4 5 6 7 8 9 0 TP 03 02 01 00 99

Cover photo by Mark M. Menard

Library of Congress Cataloging-in-Publication Data

Menard, Mark M.
    Mountain biking Chico / by Mark M. Menard.
        p. cm.—(A Falcon guide)
    Includes bibliographical references (p.) and index.
    ISBN 1-56044-804-0 (pbk. : alk. paper)
    1. All terrain cycling—California—Chico Region—Guidebooks.
2. Bicycle trails—California—Chico Region—Guidebooks. 3. Chico
Region (Calif.)—Guidebooks. I. Title. II. Series.
GV1045.5.C22C555 1999
917.94'32—dc21

CAUTION

Outdoor recreational activities are by their very nature potentially hazardous. All participants in such activities must assume the responsibility for their own actions and safety. The information contained in this guidebook cannot replace sound judgment and good decision-making skills, which help reduce risk exposure, nor does the scope of this book allow for disclosure of all the potential hazards and risks involved in such activities.

Learn as much as possible about the outdoor recreational activities in which you participate, prepare for the unexpected, and be cautious. The reward will be a safer and more enjoyable experience.

 Text pages printed on recycled paper.

Contents

Rides Near Paradise

Rides Near Chico

Acknowledgments

Writing this book was quite an adventure, facilitated by a great number of people—from avid cyclists, to park and recreation officials, to family and friends. My oldest brother, Mario, planted the seed for this book, and many others have nurtured it since then.

I am deeply indebted to Mike Peavy of Cycle Sport, both for divulging many of his favorite trails and for providing me with a great bike and excellent service.

My old roomies—Greg Calfee, Ryan Edwards, and Chris Fraze—you guys really showed me how to have fun on wheels!

Thanks to Dr. Victor Fisher and Dr. David Brown for teaching me how to read topographic maps, to understand the flow of water, and to otherwise appreciate the science behind the beauty in the marvelous processes of the earth.

Tom Barrett and Dennis Beardsley provided valuable input on Bidwell Park.

Some great company—Don Jost, John Sharpe, Jess Perez, Hillary Linke, Ron Manwill, Susan Baldwin, Karl Baumgartner, Tracy Love, Hilary Locke, Joseph O'Neil, and many others—made mountain biking a rewarding social experience.

Angel Tara Ohr came into the picture just in time to show me some favorite singletrack and a cool spot to swim.

And thanks to all the other fun guys and lovely Chico women for making this town a celebrated place to live.

USDA Forest Service employees Tricia Humpherys, Jane Goodwin, Bill Haire, and many others were surprisingly helpful allies in the crusade to make the forests safe and accessible.

Thanks also to City of Oroville Community Relations Manager Amelia Jennings and the guys at Greenline Cycles in Oroville for helping me discover the fine biking trails in Oroville.

The credit for quality maps and elevation profiles goes to my nephew, David Stewart.

Thank you, Mom and Dad, for your confidence in me.

A special thanks to my best friend, Dennis Tobin, for unwavering support and sensible advice throughout this project.

. . . and so there ain't nothing more to write about, and I am rotten glad of it, because if I'd a knowed what a trouble it was to make a book I wouldn't a tackled it and I ain't agoing to no more.

The Adventures of Huckleberry Finn, Mark Twain

MAP LEGEND

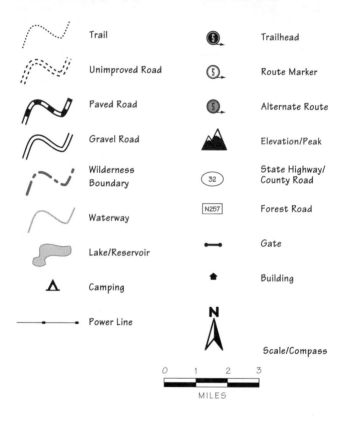

Trail	Trailhead
Unimproved Road	Route Marker
Paved Road	Alternate Route
Gravel Road	Elevation/Peak
Wilderness Boundary	State Highway/County Road
Waterway	Forest Road
Lake/Reservoir	Gate
Camping	Building
Power Line	

N

Scale/Compass

0   1   2   3

MILES

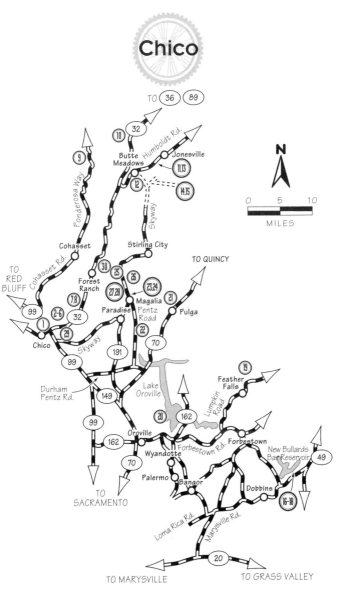

Get Ready to CRANK!

Why Chico, California? Because Chico is simply one of the best places in the world to live and bicycle: the climate is favorable to cycling most of the year; Chico's Bidwell Park is the third largest municipal park in the United States; Chico is surrounded by several large national forests; people here are fun and friendly; we have a dozen great bicycle shops; housing is cheap; the crime rate is low; and enthusiasm is high. In its August 1997 issue, *Bicycling* magazine chose Chico as the number one bicycling town in America. Come to Chico and see for yourself!

This book was written for the express purpose of getting lots of people out and enjoying nature. Rides in this book vary from the easy family ride in Lower Bidwell Park to the 37-mile trek to Black Rock Mountain alongside the Ishi Wilderness. From smooth, flat, well-paved roads, to rocky, steep, serpentine singletrack, *Mountain Biking Chico* has rides for cyclists of all levels of aerobic fitness and bike-handling skill.

How to Use This Guide

Mountain Biking Chico describes 30 mountain bike rides in their entirety. All are located in the Table of Contents, organized by geographic region. Rides are also categorized by other criteria in A Short Index of Rides. Half of the rides in this book are out-and-back routes, several are loops, and a few are out-and-back with a scenic detour or side-loop for added variety. Many of the out-and-back rides offer the choice of either returning on the same route or using an alternative return leg. A few offer a Variation for an extra leg or an easier ride.

All ride descriptions in this book use the following format:

Number and Name of the Ride: Rides are cross-referenced by number throughout this book. In many cases, parts of rides or entire routes can be linked to other rides for longer trips or variations of a standard route. These opportunities are noted, followed by "see Ride(s) #."

Names of rides are derived from official names of trails, roads, and natural features as shown on national forest and U.S. Geological Survey maps. When road naming is inconsistent amongst maps or between maps and signage, preference is given to signage and prevalence of use (for example, Camp Creek Road is labeled Pulga Road on some maps, but has a sign indicating Camp Creek Road).

Location: The general whereabouts of the ride; distance and direction from Chico.

Distance: The length of the ride in miles. Out-and-back rides are indicated as such.

Time: An estimate of how long it takes to complete the ride (for example, 1 to 2 hours). *The time listed is the actual riding time and does not include rest stops.* Strong, skilled riders may be able to do a given ride in less time, while other riders may take considerably longer. Also bear in mind that severe weather, changes in trail conditions, or mechanical problems may prolong a ride.

Tread: The type of road or trail: paved road, gravel road, dirt road or jeep track, doubletrack, and singletrack.

Aerobic level: The level of physical effort required to complete the ride: easy, moderate, or strenuous.

Easy: Flat or gently rolling terrain. No steeps or prolonged climbs.

Moderate: Some hills. Climbs may be short and fairly steep or long and gradual.

Strenuous: Frequent or prolonged climbs steep enough to require riding in the lowest gear; requires a high level of aerobic fitness, power, and endurance. Less fit riders may need to walk.

Technical difficulty: The level of bike-handling skills needed to complete the ride upright and in one piece. Technical difficulty is rated on a scale from 1 to 5 (including plus or minus symbols), with 1 being the easiest and 5 the hardest. Generally, 1 is reserved for good pavement, 2 applies to smooth gravel roads, 3 and 4 are used for rough unimproved roads and singletrack, and 5 is for expert-level singletrack or highly eroded jeep trails (-5, 5, and 5+ apply to the kind of scary stuff that often warrants getting off the bike and hiking).

Level 1: Basic bike-riding skills needed. The tread is smooth and without obstacles, ruts, or steeps.

Level 2: Mostly smooth tread; wide, well-groomed singletrack or road/doubletrack with minor ruts or loose gravel or sand.

Level 3: Irregular tread with some rough sections; singletrack or doubletrack with obvious route choices; some steep sections; occasional obstacles may include small roots, rocks, water bars, ruts, loose gravel or sand, and sharp turns or broad, open switchbacks.

Level 4: Rough tread with few smooth places; singletrack or rough doubletrack with limited route choices; steep sections, some with obstacles; obstacles are numerous and varied, including rocks, roots, branches, ruts, sidehills, narrow tread, loose gravel or sand, and switchbacks.

Level 5: Continuously broken, rocky, root-infested, or trenched tread; singletrack or extremely rough doubletrack with few route choices; frequent, sudden, and severe changes in gradient; some slopes are so steep that wheels lift off the ground; obstacles are nearly continuous and may include boulders, logs, water, large holes, deep ruts, ledges, piles of loose gravel, steep sidehills, encroaching trees, and tight switchbacks.

Hazards: A list of dangers that may be encountered on a ride, including traffic, weather, trail obstacles and conditions, risky stream crossings, obscure trails, and other perils. Remember: conditions may change at any time. Be alert for storms, new fences, downfall, missing trail signs, mechanical failure, and animals such as cougars, bears, rattlesnakes, and skunks. Also be aware of poison oak, disease-bearing ticks, and water-borne threats such as Cryptosporidium. Fatigue, heat, cold, and/or dehydration may impair judgment. Always wear a helmet and other safety equipment such as eye protection. Ride in control at all times.

Highlights: Special features or qualities that make a ride worthwhile.

Land status: A list of managing agencies or landowners. Most of the rides in this book are in national forests, state park lands, or Bidwell Park. But many of the rides also cross portions of private lands. Always leave gates as you found them. And respect the land, regardless of who owns it. See Appendix A for a list of local addresses for land-managing agencies.

Maps: A list of available maps. The following maps provide a good overview of the region covered by this book: USDA Forest Service maps for Lassen National Forest and Plumas National Forest, Cycle Sport's map of Bidwell Park, and local road maps. For adventuresome cyclists scouting the High Lakes region, relevant 7.5-minute quads and a compass should be taken on rides. Not all routes are shown on official maps.

Access: How to find the trailhead or start of the ride. Ride 29, Doe Mill Ridge, and all of the rides in Bidwell Park (Rides 1 through 8) are accessible by bike from Chico. The rest are within a 90-minute drive from Chico.

The Ride: A start-to-finish route description that correlates distance, as measured by a cyclo-computer (or bicycle odometer), with important course features, such as turns, trail junctions, landmarks, stream crossings, summits, and hazards. Although mileage is fairly accurately given to tenths of a mile, care should be taken to keep such readings in proper perspective. For example, reducing tire pressure by 25 psi can reduce the rolling radius of the wheel by as much as a centimeter, thus understating mileage by about 3 percent (or 0.3 mile for a 10-mile ride). Simply putting more weight on the front tire on a descent will be reflected in a reading which differs from that given on the climb along the exact same route. Carefully calibrating your cyclo-computer to reflect normal tire pressure and wear and making allowances for small discrepancies will help to make the most of the mileage logs in this book. Also, a small compass, clipped onto a jersey zipper, might prove invaluable for navigation—especially in remote wooded locations.

Elevation Graphs

An elevation profile accompanies each description. Here the ups and downs of the route are graphed on a grid of elevation (in feet above sea level) on the left and miles across the bottom. Route surface conditions (see map legend) and technical levels are shown on the graphs.

Note that these graphs are not scaled to perfectly reflect actual slopes. They are exaggerated vertically to call attention to the slope of the route. In short, the slope of a line on an elevation profile is generally much steeper than the actual trail surface. Also keep in mind that the ratio of elevation to distance (for vertical exaggeration) varies from graph to graph, so it's best to study each graph individually and make note of the actual distance climbed as well as the rate of climb.

I have tried to design the rides in this book so that most of the climbing is included in the first half of the ride, with the easier descent on the return. This way, a tired rider has the option of cutting a ride short without getting trapped in a topographical hole. However, several rides in this book do include steep out-and-back routes where the gravitational potential energy is spent before it is earned (you roll downhill going out and climb back). Be realistic when contemplating these rides on your first attempt.

IMBA Rules of the Trail

Responsible, thoughtful cyclists can help foster good will and ensure the future of mountain biking by observing a few simple practices. In addition to refraining from undesirable acts like littering and riding on property that is posted against trespassing, a good mountain biker should also take positive action. Volunteering time for trail maintenance is a good way to meet civic-minded cyclists as well as improve a favorite trail. And being extra friendly and courteous to all the equestrians, hikers, rangers, and others on the trails makes for a more pleasant day for all and a better future for mountain biking. Please do your part to promote this wonderful sport by observing the following guidelines put forth by the International Mountain Biking Association (IMBA):

1. Ride on open trails only. Respect trail and road closures (ask if not sure), avoid possible trespass on private land, obtain permits and authorization as may be required. Federal and state wilderness areas are closed to cycling. The way you ride will influence trail management decisions and policies.

2. Leave no trace. Be sensitive to the dirt beneath you. Even on open (legal) trails, you should not ride under conditions where you will leave evidence of your passing, such as on certain soils after a rain. Recognize different types of soil and trail construction; practice low-impact cycling. This also means staying on existing trails and not creating any new ones. Be sure to pack out at least as much as you pack in.

3. Control your bicycle! Inattention for even a second can cause problems. Obey all bicycle speed regulations and recommendations.

4. Always yield trail. Make known your approach well in advance. A friendly greeting (or bell) is considerate and works well; don't startle others. Show your respect when passing by slowing to a walking pace or stopping. Anticipate other trail users at corners and blind spots.

5. Never spook animals. All animals are startled by an unannounced approach, a sudden movement, or a loud noise. This can be dangerous for you, others, and the animals. Give animals extra time and room to adjust to you. When passing horses use special care and follow directions from the horseback riders (dismount and ask if uncertain). Running cattle and disturbing wildlife is a serious offense. Leave gates as you found them, or as marked.

6. Plan ahead. Know your equipment, your ability, and the area in which you are riding—and prepare accordingly. Be self-sufficient at all times, keep your equipment in good repair, and carry necessary supplies for changes in weather or other conditions. A well-executed trip is a satisfaction to you and not a burden or offense to others. Always wear a helmet.

Keep trails open by setting a good example of environmentally sound and socially responsible off-road cycling.

Be Prepared

Mountain biking out in the countryside can be a very rewarding experience. It can also turn out to be unpleasant or downright ugly if you overlook certain precautions and preparations. Natural threats such as poison oak, Lyme disease, rattlesnakes, mountain lions, and heat exhaustion, as well as mechanical problems, are largely avoidable with adequate preparation. The following is an overview of some of the problems particular to the Chico area that should be taken seriously.

Poison oak (*Toxicodendron diversilobum*) is found in most of the areas covered by this guide. Although many people enjoy varying degrees of immunity to this plant, some are very sensitive to its powerful skin irritant. Poison oak grows either as a small shrub, 3 to 8 feet tall, or as a vine, climbing the trunks and branches of shrubs and trees. It is identifiable by its pattern of leaves—three oval-to-round leaflets per sprig—glossy on top, with a duller, paler underside. Leaves are lobed, 2 to 3 inches long, and green most of the year. In autumn they turn red, and white fruits appear. Even casual contact with the oil of these leaves can cause severe rashes and other medical complications. If you do come in contact with poison oak, gently wash the affected area with cool water and soap. See your physician or pharmacist for additional information and treatment.

Lyme disease, although rare in this area, is a serious threat, and should be considered. It is caused by Lyme disease spirochetes (*Borrelia burgdorferi*) carried by western black-legged ticks or deer ticks and is transmitted by tick bites. These small, eight-legged pests are red-brown to brownish black, about 1/8-inch long. They can be found on grasses and brush, waiting on the tips of plants, often along animal paths or trails. When an unsuspecting animal (such as a mountain biker) brushes against the plant, these blood-sucking hitchhikers latch on and bite their host. You can reduce the risk of transmission of Lyme disease by removing the tick as soon as possible. Use tweezers or forceps to carefully grasp the tick—including its small head—and pull directly out (no twisting). Hot oil and other folklore methods are not recommended. Although only 2 to 3 percent of deer ticks in this area carry this disease, you may wish to have a local lab test any ticks you find embedded, as prompt treatment is essential. Save and transport suspect ticks in a small watertight container with a couple of drops of water. After each ride, carefully check your clothing and body for these parasites.

A more obvious threat is posed by the western rattlesnake, or northern Pacific rattler. Rather than getting a close look at a suspected snake's markings to determine its species, it is preferable to move out of striking distance (usually about 7 feet), and look for the distinctive triangular head of these vipers.

Remember that even a baby less than a foot long can be as venomous as a 5-foot adult. Because of the fairly large population of rattlesnakes in this area, consider carrying an inexpensive snakebite kit on all rides (except during winter). If you are so unfortunate as to receive a bite, seek immediate medical attention. Although rattlesnake bites are not often fatal, they do cause severe tissue damage and can result in the loss of a limb or other serious complications.

A much larger threat, the mountain lion or cougar, is seldom encountered in this area, yet can be very aggressive and dangerous. An adult male can weigh as much as 150 pounds and may be quite hungry when you meet him. In the unlikely event that you are confronted by a mountain lion, the following suggestions could save you from severe injury or death.

- Don't charge toward it or run away.
- Stand tall and make eye contact.
- Spread your arms (or lift your bicycle up over your head) and speak firmly and loudly.
- Gather your children; don't bend over to pick them up.
- Slowly back away from the lion, facing it at all times.
- If attacked, fight back with whatever weapons are at hand: sticks, rocks, your bicycle, or backpack.
- Try to stay standing.

The important thing to remember is that you want to appear as a large, upright, formidable opponent rather than a small, four-legged animal similar to normal prey.

Another important concern while mountain biking in the Chico region is blazing summertime sun. Temperatures here often exceed 100 degrees F. Bringing enough water for a longer ride might mean bringing a gallon or more! Typically, 20 to 50 ounces per hour of riding is recommended for a hot day. Also consider wearing sunblock and a visor or sunglasses.

Although it is difficult to predict what kind of mechanical failure might be in store for any ride, careful routine bicycle maintenance goes a long way toward making your experience out in nature safe and comfortable. Here's my list of items for routine rides: spare tube, pump, tire levers, tire patch kit, and a multi-tool (which includes flat and phillips screwdrivers, several allen wrenches, spoke wrench, and a few common box and open-ended wrenches). For personal maintenance I also put a small compass, toilet tissue, sunblock, and a snakebite kit into a mountain biking knapsack with 100 ounces of water, a banana, and a couple of energy bars.

Lower Bidwell Park

Location: Lower Bidwell Park in central Chico.

Distance: 8.6-mile loop.

Time: 30 minutes to 1 hour.

Tread: 8.6 miles on paved road and paved bike path; 2.5 miles on optional singletrack.

Aerobic level: Easy; all flat.

Technical difficulty: 1 on pavement; 2 and 2+ on singletrack.

Hazards: Paved roads are open to automobile traffic during the day; feral cats dart in front of cyclists at night. To prevent automobile traffic, heavy steel gates are closed from one hour after sunset until 11 A.M. This may be an important consideration when racing home to dinner in an unlit park.

Highlights: Nice, scenic park setting. Good pavement canopied by large oak and sycamore trees throughout. Sycamore Pool and a large picnic area are located at One Mile Recreational Area. Although this ride is not a mountain biking ride per se, it offers a wonderful riparian setting and serves as a great warm-up leading into Upper Park. And there are some fast, fun little stretches of singletrack available on the return portion of the ride.

Land status: City of Chico park.

Maps: City of Chico Parks Department.

Access: The entire ride is within Chico city limits and is accessible from numerous spots. Start from the north parking lot at

• Lower Bidwell Park

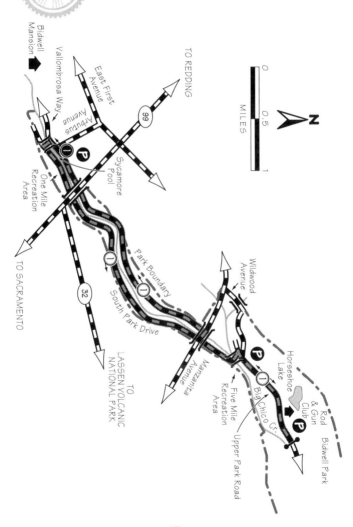

One Mile Recreational Area (so called because of its distance from historic Bidwell Mansion), just a few yards east of the corner of Vallombrosa Way and Vallombrosa Avenue. There is additional parking on the south side of One Mile Recreational Area. One Mile is a great place to picnic and has a creek-fed public swimming pool open during the warmer months.

The Ride

0.0   From the parking lot on Vallombrosa Way, head south 150 yards and walk your bike across the footbridge to a paved path. Pedal south 100 yards to a junction and turn left. You'll be sharing this path with small children, dogs, cats, and senior citizens, so please ride accordingly.

0.1   Restrooms on your left.

0.3   The paved path branches again. Turn left and head northeast alongside Big Chico Creek for the next 4 miles. None of the dirt paths on the south side of Big Chico Creek in Lower Bidwell Park are open to bicycles (except for one short stretch at One Mile Recreational Area).

0.5   Bear left—stay on the paved path—and pass under California Highway 99.

0.7   Turn left onto a wide, one-way path. Stay on the right side of path.

1.6	Turn left on South Park Drive. Watch for automobile traffic.
2.6	Stop sign. Stay left onto a green paved path. Watch for equestrian traffic.
2.9	Cross Manzanita Avenue. Stay on the green paved path.
3.2	Five Mile Recreational Area. Ignore the bridge on the left and bear right.
3.3	Walk your bike across a footbridge just past the restrooms on the left. Go right on the paved road beyond the gravel parking area.
3.6	You are now in Upper Bidwell Park. Turn right on Wildwood Avenue. Take note of the North Rim Trail parking area on the left. This is the staging area for Ride 4, Middle Trail, and Ride 5, North Rim Trail.
3.7	Cross the street and roll onto a pedestrian/bicycle path.
4.1	Horseshoe Lake parking area on the left.
4.3	Chico Rod and Gun Club on left. The bike path ends and merges onto a paved road.
4.4	Stop at a steel gate. This is the start of Ride 2, Upper Park Road. Note the singletrack and signpost in the northwest corner of parking area. This is the trailhead for Ride 3, Lower Trail. Retrace your route back to Manzanita Avenue (at mile 2.9, above).
6.0	Turn right over Big Chico Creek and, heeding traffic, go left across Manzanita Avenue onto the paved path on the north side of the creek.
6.2	The path merges onto North Park Drive. Watch for cars, and pedal southwest.
6.6	Note the singletrack on your left. This is one of several stretches on the creek side of North Park Drive that takes off and rejoins the paved road. Dirt trails on the right are closed to cyclists.
8.6	Welcome back to the start and your car.

Upper Park Road

Location: Upper Bidwell Park, 5 miles northeast of downtown Chico.

Distance: 8.2 miles, out and back.

Time: 1 to 2 hours, round trip.

Tread: 0.4 mile on paved road; 2.8 miles on gravel road; 5 miles on rough unimproved road.

Aerobic level: Easy to moderate.

Technical difficulty: 1 on pavement; 2 on gravel road; 3 on unimproved road.

Hazards: Large rocks and ruts on the unimproved road. Water bars/speed bumps are added and changed seasonally, and are sometimes radical enough to make a fast descent unwise. Watch your speed on the unimproved road—it's easy to reach unsafe speeds on rough, curvy stretches.

Highlights: Dramatic basalt cliffs at Devil's Kitchen. Beautiful views and swimming holes at Alligator Hole, Bear Hole, Salmon Hole, and Brown's Hole. When Upper Bidwell Park trails are closed due to rains, Upper Park Road is open to cyclists who aren't averse to mud.

Land status: City of Chico park.

Maps: Cycle Sport; City of Chico Parks Department; USGS 7.5-minute quads for Richardson Springs, Paradise West.

Access: From California Highway 99, exit east on East Avenue. Drive 2.6 miles (East Avenue becomes Manzanita Avenue) and

Upper Park Road

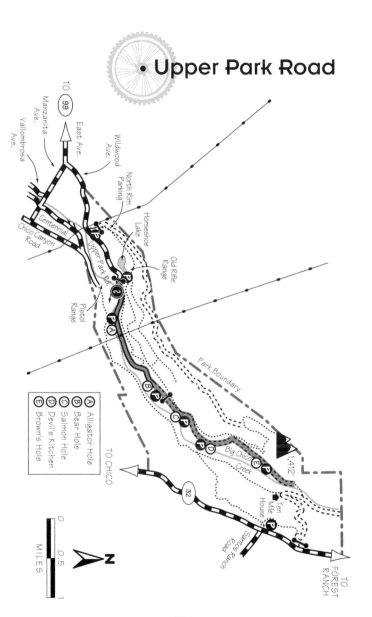

Legend:
- Ⓐ Alligator Hole
- Ⓑ Bear Hole
- Ⓒ Salmon Hole
- Ⓓ Devil's Kitchen
- Ⓔ Brown's Hole

TO 99
Manzanita Ave.
Vallombrosa Ave.
East Ave.
Wildwood Ave.
North Rim Parking
Horseshoe Lake
Old Rifle Range
Centennial
Chico Canyon Road
Upper Park Rd.
Pistol Range
Park Boundary
Big Chico Creek
1,412'
TO CHICO
32
Ten Mile House
Santos Ranch Road
TO FOREST RANCH

MILES
0   0.5   1

N

turn left (northeast) onto Wildwood Avenue. Drive 1.6 miles on Wildwood Avenue (which becomes Upper Park Road after 0.25 mile) and park in the lot on the left just before a steel gate. Alternatively, by parking at One Mile Recreational Area, this ride may be combined with Ride 1 (Lower Bidwell Park) for an overall distance of 16.8 miles.

The Ride

0.0 Ride officially begins here at the steel gate, just past Horseshoe Lake and the Chico Rod and Gun Club. Pedal east on the paved road.

0.2 Stop sign. Pause to read the large sign listing park rules, including the helmet requirement. The road here changes from pavement to gravel, which is sometimes rough, requiring basic off-road skills.

0.2 Alligator Hole scenic creek area may be accessed here. As with the entire area between Upper Park Road and Big Chico Creek, bicycling is prohibited except on automobile access roads.

0.7 Power lines overhead.

1.6 Bear Hole parking area. An emergency phone is located here. (Portable toilets are also available during warmer

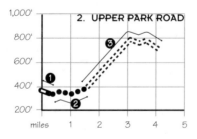

months.) The road becomes less of a gravel road and gets a little rougher here (2+).

2.1 Salmon Hole parking area.

2.6 Devil's Kitchen parking area—a good place to stop and appreciate the steep basalt cliffs created by the creek's erosion over millions of years. Enjoy the view of the opposing cliffs covered with moss, lichens, and trees reaching over the water 200 feet below.

3.1 Watch out for a 200-foot section of loose cobbles and boulders (rated a 3).

3.2 The road descends for about 0.2 mile, then climbs again.

4.1 End of Upper Park Road. (The singletrack at the road's end continues for a hundred yards or so, then branches right for a creek crossing and left to a hiking trail.)

The creek is close to the road at this point and offers a chance for a quiet observer to see great blue herons. Turn around and enjoy a return ride that drops about 400 feet from Brown's Hole to the steel gate at the start. And remember that those speed bumps can change your mountain bike ride into a circus act!

8.2 Back at the steel gate.

Lower Trail

Location: Upper Bidwell Park, 5 miles northeast of downtown Chico.

Distance: 2.7-mile loop.

Time: 20 to 40 minutes.

Tread: 1.3 miles on singletrack; 1.4 miles on gravel road.

Aerobic level: Easy to moderate.

Technical difficulty: Mostly 2 and 3, with several short technical sections (4) on singletrack; 2 on gravel road.

Hazards: Unanticipated fixed rocks can stop a front wheel and send you head over heels. Loose cobbles and boulders of all sizes threaten to undermine your balance. Poison oak can be thick on the Lower Trail, depending on seasonal changes and trail maintenance.

Highlights: Trail winds through pretty setting of grass-covered hills and oak trees, with several challenging rocky technical sections.

Land status: City of Chico park.

Maps: Cycle Sport; City of Chico Parks Department; USGS 7.5-minute quad for Richardson Springs.

Access: From California Highway 99, exit east on East Avenue. Drive 2.6 miles (East Avenue becomes Manzanita Avenue) and turn left (northeast) onto Wildwood Avenue. Drive 1.6 miles on Wildwood Avenue (which becomes Upper Park Road after 0.2 mile) and park in the parking lot on the left, just before a steel

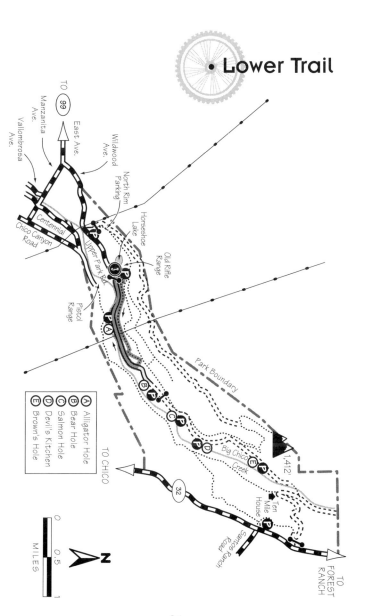

• Lower Trail

TO 99
Marzanita Ave.
Vallombrosa Ave.
East Ave.
Wildwood Ave.
North Rim Parking
Centennial
Chico Canyon Road
Upper Park Rd.
Pistol Range
Horseshoe Lake
Old Rifle Range

Park Boundary

TO CHICO
32

Big Chico Creek
Santos Ranch Road
Ten Mile House
1,412'

TO FOREST RANCH

A Alligator Hole
B Bear Hole
C Salmon Hole
D Devil's Kitchen
E Brown's Hole

MILES
0   0.5   1

N

21

gate. Alternatively, by parking at One Mile Recreational Area, this ride may be combined with Ride 1 (Lower Bidwell Park) for an overall distance of 11.3 miles.

The Ride

0.0 Begin at the northeast corner of the parking lot near the old rifle range (just past the Chico Rod and Gun Club on Upper Park Road).

0.1 Cross a small ravine on an old concrete footbridge. Bear right at an upcoming fork in the trail.

0.2 Go left at a signpost.

0.3 Caution—technical sections with lots of rocks (call them a 4).

0.5 Enjoy flat, smooth singletrack.

0.9 Roll into a tree-covered grassy area. Look for owls and other woodland birds.

1.0 Jam up a short but steep technical climb.

1.1 Bump through one of several rocky gullies on the Lower Trail. Just ahead the doubletrack splits into two singletrack trails; go left.

1.2 Go right at a Y junction. (The Lower Trail closely parallels Upper Park Road for the most part.)

1.3 Trail ends at Upper Park Road. Take Upper Park Road to the right for an easier, faster return.

2.7 Back where you started.

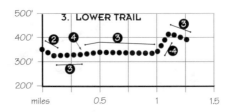

Middle Trail

Location: Upper Bidwell Park, 5 miles northeast of downtown Chico.

Distance: 8.4-mile loop.

Time: 1 to 2 hours.

Tread: 1 mile on paved road; 1.4 miles on gravel road; 1.7 miles on unimproved road; 4.3 miles on singletrack.

Aerobic level: Easy to moderate.

Technical difficulty: 1 on pavement; 2 on gravel; 3 on unimproved road; 3 and 4 on singletrack.

Hazards: Unanticipated fixed rocks can stop a front wheel and send you head over heels. Loose cobbles and boulders of all sizes threaten to undermine your balance. Water bars/speed bumps on Upper Park Road designed by launch-crazy NASA rocket scientists. Poison oak can be thick on the Middle Trail, depending on seasonal changes and trail maintenance.

Highlights: Challenging technical sections (especially rocky gullies) and plenty of natural scenery, including oak trees, grassy hills, diverse geologic formations, hawks, owls, and a surprising variety of other wildlife.

Land status: City of Chico park.

Maps: Cycle Sport; City of Chico Parks Department; USGS 7.5-minute quads for Richardson Springs, Paradise West.

Access: From California Highway 99, exit east on East Avenue. Drive 2.6 miles (East Avenue becomes Manzanita Avenue) and

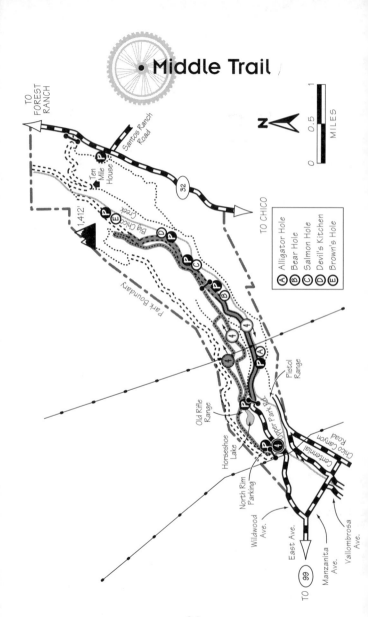

Middle Trail

MILES
0   0.5   1

N

TO FOREST RANCH

Samos Ranch Road

Ten Mile House

P

32

TO CHICO

1,412'

Big Chico Creek

E

D

P

C

B

P

A

4

4

Park Boundary

Old Rifle Range

Pistol Range

Horseshoe Lake

North Rim Parking

Upper Park Rd.

Centennial

Chico Canyon Road

4

P

P

Wildwood Ave.

East Ave.

Manzanita Ave.

Vallombrosa Ave.

TO 99

(A) Alligator Hole
(B) Bear Hole
(C) Salmon Hole
(D) Devil's Kitchen
(E) Brown's Hole

24

turn left (northeast) onto Wildwood Avenue. Drive 0.9 mile on Wildwood Avenue (which becomes Upper Park Road after 0.2 mile) and park in North Rim parking lot on the left. Alternatively, by parking at One Mile Recreational Area, this ride may be combined with Ride 1 (Lower Bidwell Park) for an overall distance of 13.1 miles.

The Ride

0.0 Begin at the gate at the end of the North Rim parking area. In about 50 yards the trail branches left as doubletrack and right as singletrack. Take the singletrack to the right.

0.1 Stay to the right at a signpost. The trail here is fairly level, smooth singletrack overlooking a small meadow and passing north of Horseshoe Lake.

0.5 Continue northeast across a trail that heads toward Horseshoe Lake. In another 100 yards or so (about halfway past the lake), the trail forks. Take the middle route.

0.7 Another trail crossing; stay on the middle course, heading north-northeast.

0.8 Take the lowest of three branches on a northeast heading. You are now right in the middle of a rifle range. Don't worry, though, it has been closed for a long time.

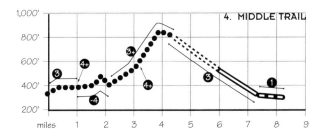

0.9 Technical section (4) through a rocky gully, just after the shooting range parking area. Here you have a choice of three trails. The trail to the left is a hiking trail. Straight ahead is the Upper Middle Trail (see the variation below), a very technical ride. Take the trail to the right to continue on the Middle Trail. From this point on, the trail becomes rocky and climbs moderately. Watch out for both fixed rocks and loose cobbles and boulders.

1.0 Stay left; merge onto a wider singletrack, heading east. Continue 100 yards to another fork.

1.1 Take the lower branch to the right at the fork.

1.3 Go right at a Y junction.

1.6 Power lines overhead.

2.1 Rocky gully.

3.0 Go left at another Y, heading northwest. (This ride can be reduced 2.5 miles by turning right here, then right just ahead onto Upper Park Road.)

3.2 Bounce through a short rocky section (4+).

3.9 Negotiate a small ravine.

4.2 A sharp, short drop in the trail requires care. In 25 yards, turn right at a T intersection, heading downhill. This is the lowest portion of the North Rim descent.

4.3 Turn right on Upper Park Road and run south and west for the next 4 miles.

8.4 North Rim parking area.

Variation: The Upper Middle Trail offers a more technical ride with another 200 feet of climbing. Follow the above route until you reach the trail junction at 0.9 mile. Take the center trail and cinch down your helmet.

1.0 Bear left onto a merging trail.

1.4 Trail branches; keep right. Work through a challenging little ravine. In about 30 yards bear left, crossing beneath power lines.

1.5 Very difficult gully to get through without dabbing. Good luck!

1.9 Hang a right where the trail branches by a huge boulder. This monolith is about 7 feet tall and is probably some kind of omen for the foolhardy cyclist who continues to the left. The trail quickly descends until it ties into Middle Trail.

2.1 Go left onto the Middle Trail on a northeast heading.

2.4 The trail begins to climb more seriously. You're back on the Middle Trail, following the ride description above.

North Rim Trail

Location: Upper Bidwell Park, 5 miles northeast of downtown Chico.

Distance: 9.2-mile loop.

Time: 1 to 2 hours.

Tread: 1 mile on paved road; 1.4 miles on gravel road; 1.7 miles on unimproved road; 3.6 miles on service road; 1.5 miles on singletrack.

Aerobic level: Moderate.

Technical difficulty: Mostly 3 and 4 with a couple of mean (5) switchbacks on the descent.

Hazards: Unanticipated fixed rocks can stop a front wheel and send you head over heels. Loose cobbles and boulders of all sizes threaten to undermine your balance; there are several

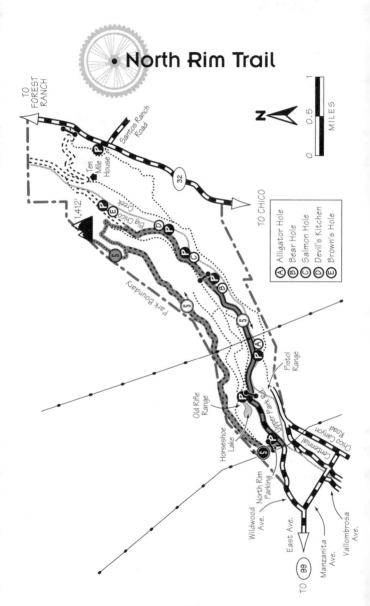

North Rim Trail

TO FOREST RANCH

Santos Ranch Road

Ten Mile House

32

TO CHICO

Ⓐ Alligator Hole
Ⓑ Bear Hole
Ⓒ Salmon Hole
Ⓓ Devils Kitchen
Ⓔ Brown's Hole

MILES
0   0.5   1

N

1,412'

Big Chico Creek

Park Boundary

Old Rifle Range

Horseshoe Lake

North Rim Parking

Wildwood Ave.

Upper Park Rd.

Pistol Range

Centennial

Chico Canyon Road

East Ave.

Manzanita Ave.

Vallombrosa Ave.

TO 99

steep, tight, rocky switchbacks that get trickier each year. Poison oak can be thick on the North Rim Descent, depending on seasonal changes and trail maintenance.

Highlights: Panoramic views of the greater Chico metropolitan area, if you choose to look back. Views of valleys and ridges left and right, overlooking the park during most of the climb. Exciting and challenging North Rim descent.

Land status: City of Chico park.

Maps: Cycle Sport; City of Chico Parks Department; USGS 7.5-minute quads for Richardson Springs, Paradise West.

Access: From California Highway 99, exit east on East Avenue. Drive 2.6 miles (East Avenue becomes Manzanita Avenue) and turn left (northeast) onto Wildwood Avenue. Drive 0.9 mile on Wildwood Avenue (which becomes Upper Park Road after 0.2 mile) and park in the North Rim parking lot on the left. Alternatively, by parking at One Mile Recreational Area, this ride may be combined with Ride 1 (Lower Bidwell Park) for an overall distance of 16.5 miles.

The Ride

0.0 Begin at the gate at the end of the North Rim parking area. In about 50 yards the trail branches left as a service road (wide doubletrack) and right as singletrack. Keep left and take a deep breath—you will climb about 800 feet through lots and lots of rocks in the next 3.6 miles.

0.3 This barbed-wire fence is the northern park boundary. Follow the service road to the right.

0.7 For a nice view of the city, stop and look over your shoulder.

0.8 The trail gets rockier from this point on until the North Rim Descent.

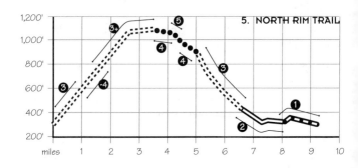

0.9 Go left at a signpost.

1.2 The trail begins a steeper climb.

1.6 Power lines overhead.

2.0 Look around and enjoy the peace and quiet.

2.2 The trail moves over to the north side of the park's northern rim.

2.6 Gear down for a steep climb.

3.1 Look up to the right to see the outcropping known as Monkeyface.

3.6 Turn right at a signpost to begin down the North Rim Descent, also called B Trail, or Live Oak Trail. (Riders who are allergic to poison oak or averse to technical riding may wish to turn around and head back at this point.) Descent is fairly narrow singletrack much of the way. The next 1.5 miles can be a lot of fun for an alert and reasonable rider. There is no shame in walking through any of the upcoming technical switchbacks.

4.0 The trail narrows and becomes rockier (4).

4.1 Slow down for a tight switchback to the right, then another switchback to the left, known to some locals as Blood Rock (5).

4.4 Another tight switchback goes left, followed by a rocky stretch.

4.5 Yet another technical switchback goes left (4+). The trail gets smoother and straighter from here down to Upper Park Road.

5.0 Here we go through the brush. Keep up some speed for short climbs.

5.1 The trail branches; keep left. In about 100 yards the trail ends at Upper Park Road, about 0.5 mile north of Devil's Kitchen. Turn right on Upper Park Road and enjoy a fast return to the North Rim parking area. Watch out for rocky, washed-out sections of road and water bars/speed bumps. Also be wary of automobiles and other traffic. (See Ride 2 for a description of Upper Park Road.)

9.2 Turn right into the North Rim parking area, back where you started.

South Rim Trail

Location: South side of Upper Bidwell Park, 5 miles northeast of downtown Chico.

Distance: 9.8 miles, out and back.

Time: 1.5 to 3 hours.

Tread: 1 mile on paved road; 0.6 mile on gravel road; 8.2 miles on singletrack.

Aerobic level: Mostly moderate with a couple of strenuous climbs.

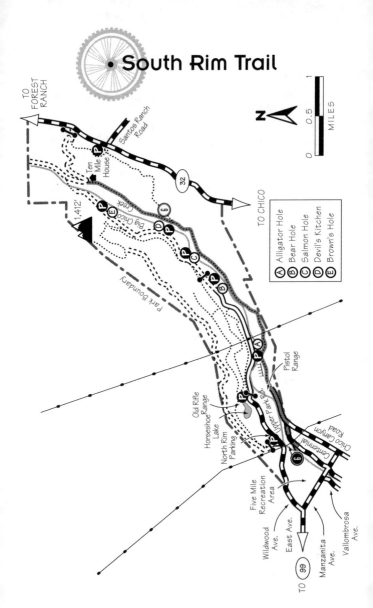

South Rim Trail

TO FOREST RANCH

TO CHICO

Santos Ranch Road

Ten Mile House

1,412'

Big Chico Creek

Park Boundary

32

Ⓐ Alligator Hole
Ⓑ Bear Hole
Ⓒ Salmon Hole
Ⓓ Devil's Kitchen
Ⓔ Brown's Hole

Pistol Range

Old Rifle Range

Horseshoe Lake

North Rim Parking

Upper Park Rd.

Centennial

Chico Canyon Road

Five Mile Recreation Area

Wildwood Ave.

East Ave.

Manzanita Ave.

Vallombrosa Ave.

TO 99

MILES
0   0.5   1

N

Technical difficulty: 1 on pavement; 2 on gravel road; 3 to 5+ on singletrack.

Hazards: Section of narrow trail next to steep cliff. Rocky, off-camber, technical sections. Short but very steep washed-out sections that must be walked. Poison oak, depending on seasonal changes and trail maintenance.

Highlights: Scenic ride on South Rim includes unmatched views of Bear Hole and Devil's Kitchen; superlative views of lowlands and coastal range as seen throughout the length of the canyon. Some of the most difficult technical climbs in Bidwell Park.

Land status: City of Chico park.

Maps: Cycle Sport; City of Chico Parks Department; USGS 7.5-minute quads for Richardson Springs, Paradise West.

Access: From California Highway 99, exit east on East Avenue and drive 3.1 miles (East Avenue becomes Manzanita Avenue). Turn left onto Centennial Avenue, drive 0.3 mile northeast, and turn left into the Five Mile Area parking lot. The ride begins on a paved path by the restrooms.

The Ride

0.0 Pedal north on the paved path/service road until you reach a steel gate.

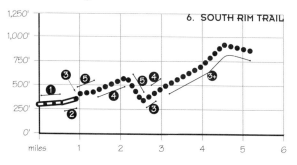

0.1 Turn left onto Centennial Avenue.

0.5 Go left past the steel gate onto a gravel service road, heading east-northeast.

0.8 Take note of the park sign posting whether the trail is open to cyclists. (Mountain biking on South Rim Trail when it is wet or muddy causes serious erosion and may result in broken bones and hefty fines.)

0.9 Singletrack begins at the northeast end of a defunct pistol range. Steep rocky sections ahead.

1.0 Rock ledge—very tough (5) to climb. Be wary of slick, off-camber rocks and devilish crevices ahead. Sensible riders may wish to walk through trouble spots.

1.2 CAUTION: Steep cliff to the left of narrow singletrack. Walk your bike if you have any reservations about this type of hazard.

1.5 Powerlines overhead. Another 120 feet of climbing brings you near the park's southern boundary.

1.9 Barbed-wire fence on the right. CAUTION: Trail soon drops abruptly, with branches, roots, ruts, and rocks challenging the most skilled riders (5+). Riders on this trail for the first time should dismount and walk next 0.3 mile.

2.0 A large pine tree may still be lying across the path when you reach this point. The trail drops 200 feet in the next 0.2 mile! Be prepared for extremely technical sections (5+), including tall ledges and a minefield of loose cobbles and boulders. (Just imagine yourself climbing that section on the return!)

2.2 Now you can relax and enjoy the scenery for a while.

2.3 Begin a moderate climb along Big Chico Creek.

2.4 You are now above Bear Hole, a great spot to swim and sunbathe. The trail gets a little trickier, with plenty of loose cobbles.

2.6 Pass through an old stacked stone fence. The boulders in that fence are from ancient lava mudflows which comprise the upper layer of Bidwell Park's geology. This layer, known as the Tuscan Formation, rests upon an older lava flow named the Lovejoy Basalt. This layer of shiny black rock rests on an even older layer of ocean sediment, the Chico Formation. You'll come to appreciate the Lovejoy Basalt when you reach Devil's Kitchen.

2.8 Pass through a rocky meadow with fewer rocks and easier going. Tall cliffs to the right.

3.1 Salmon Hole below.

3.4 Enjoy the beautiful canyon view to the left. Notice the basalt cliffs, distinguished by columnar jointing that occurred when the molten basalt lava cooled into pentagonal and hexagonal columns. Large blocks of this basalt have broken away and tumbled down to where the creek has reached down to the Chico Formation and eroded it, undermining the Lovejoy Basalt.

3.6 Devil's Kitchen to the left.

4.4 The trail reaches its highest point here, about 900 feet above sea level.

4.9 An old shack on the right is known as Ten Mile House. The trail ends in just a few yards where it meets Ten Mile House Trail. Turn around at Ten Mile House Trail (an unimproved road) and have fun retracing your tracks!

9.8 Back at Five Mile Recreational Area parking lot.

Ten Mile House Road

Location: Upper Bidwell Park, 10 miles northeast of downtown Chico.

Distance: 7.1 miles one way.

Time: 40 minutes to 1 hour.

Tread: 1.2 miles on paved road; 0.2 mile on gravel road; 5.5 miles on unimproved road; 0.2 mile on singletrack.

Aerobic level: Easy for the most part, with a couple of relatively short, moderate climbs.

Technical difficulty: 1 on pavement; 2 on gravel road; 3 to -4 on singletrack and dirt road.

Hazards: Ten Mile House Road is a very steep dirt road; excessive speeds can be reached quickly without even pedaling. Watch for pedestrians, equestrians, and automobile traffic after you cross the creek. Automobile traffic is heaviest on Saturdays. (The gate at the shooting range is locked on Upper Park Road on Sundays and after dark.) Bicyclists are required by local ordinance and common sense to wear helmets in Upper Bidwell Park.

Highlights: This is an easy, fast, fun, scenic ride.

Land status: City of Chico park.

Maps: Cycle Sport; City of Chico Parks Department; USGS 7.5-minute quads for Paradise West, Richardson Springs.

Access: This ride requires a shuttle. From California Highway 99, exit east on East Avenue. Drive 3.1 miles (East Avenue

• Ten Mile House Road

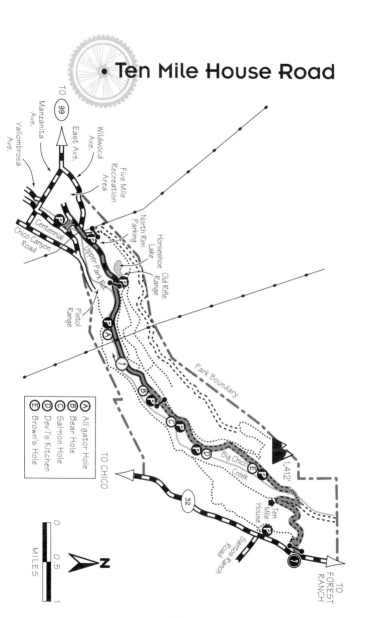

TO (99)

Manzanita Ave.
Vallombrosa Ave.
East Ave.
Wildwood Ave.

Five Mile Recreation Area

North Rim Parking

Centennial

Chico Canyon Road

Upper Park Rd.

Horseshoe Lake

Old Rifle Range

Pistol Range

Park Boundary

(A) Alligator Hole
(B) Bear Hole
(C) Salmon Hole
(D) Dev's Kitchen
(E) Brown's Hole

TO CHICO

Big Chico Creek

1,412'

32

Sanos Ranch Road

Ten Mile House

TO FOREST RANCH

MILES

0   0.5   1

N

becomes Manzanita Avenue) and turn left onto Centennial Avenue. Drive 0.3 mile northeast on Centennial and turn left into the Five Mile Area parking lot. Park one vehicle here. In a second vehicle, drive back out to Manzanita Avenue and turn left. Drive 1.2 miles on Manzanita Avenue (which becomes Bruce Road) and turn left on CA 32. Drive 6.7 miles northeast on CA 32 to Ten Mile House Road and park in the dirt parking area with a green gate on the left.

The Ride

0.0 Carry your bike over the hinged side of the locked green steel gate. The gate is locked to keep motor vehicles out. The locals usually refer to this ride as "Greengate." Check your brakes, cinch your helmet, and let 'er fly. The road gets rough (-4) in about 0.25 mile.

1.2 A large (about 10 feet high) basalt rock stands on the right. Notice the singletrack trail and old wooden shack on the left. These are, respectively, the South Rim Trail

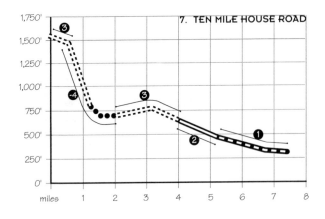

(see Ride 6) and historic Ten Mile House. Continue down Ten Mile House Road.

1.3 The tread becomes rocky again (-4) from here to the creek.

1.5 Take a sharp left onto singletrack, heading southwest.

1.6 Turn right at a Y junction and cross Big Chico Creek. After portaging across the creek, pick up singletrack on a southwest heading. Plow through some sand and a short rocky (-4) section.

1.7 The singletrack dumps onto Upper Park Road. Continue south and begin a moderate climb.

2.7 Fast downhill stretch ahead. Watch out for hikers, joggers and cars.

5.9 Pass by a road gate.

6.0 Pass by the Chico Rod and Gun Club and pick up a paved bike path.

6.7 The paved bike path ends. Continue south 50 yards past North Rim parking area and turn left onto a paved road.

7.0 Turn left into the parking area and walk across a footbridge. Telephone, toilets, and drinking water are available to your right.

7.1 Back at Five Mile Recreational Area parking lot.

Pine Trail

Location: Upper Bidwell Park, 10 miles northeast of downtown Chico.

Distance: 4.8-mile loop.

Time: 1 hour.

Tread: 1 mile on unimproved road; 3.8 miles on singletrack.

Aerobic level: Moderate, with two strenuous climbs.

Technical difficulty: The steep descents on this ride demand good timing, balance, and control (4+), otherwise averaging 3+.

Hazards: I came across a 3-foot rattlesnake while documenting this ride. It was coiled for action, but quickly retreated as I waited from a reasonable distance. The descent involves some steep, tight switchbacks with loose dirt and rocks. One section of the ride (on the South Rim Trail) is narrow and drops off precipitously on the downslope side.

Highlights: This is a challenging ride, both technically and aerobically. It is located in the least-used region of Bidwell Park, promising both beauty and solitude.

Land status: City of Chico park.

Maps: Cycle Sport; City of Chico Parks Department; USGS 7.5-minute quad for Paradise West.

Access: From California Highway 99, drive 7.9 miles east on CA 32 and park in the small clearing on the left (northwest) side of the highway, opposite Santos Ranch Road. The trailhead is 50 feet west of CA 32 (opposite Santos Ranch Road).

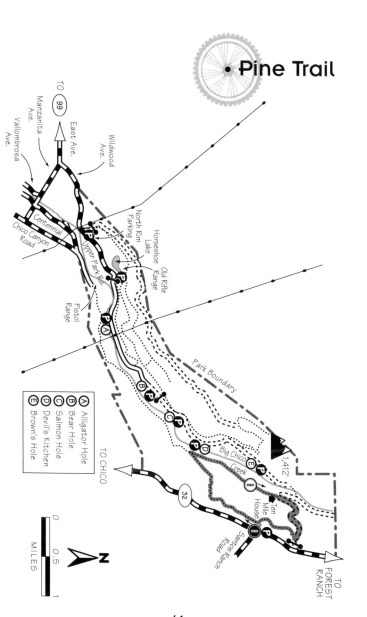

Pine Trail

TO 99
Manzanita Ave.
Vallombrosa Ave.
East Ave.
Wildwood Ave.
Centennial
Chico Canyon Road
Upper Park Rd.
North Rim Parking
Horseshoe Lake
Old Rifle Range
Pistol Range
Park Boundary
1,412'
Big Chico Creek
Ten Mile House
TO CHICO
32
Santos Ranch Road
TO FOREST RANCH

A Alligator Hole
B Bear Hole
C Salmon Hole
D Devil's Kitchen
E Brown's Hole

N

MILES
0   0.5   1

41

The Ride

0.0 Catch the singletrack at the trailhead. Prepare for steep descent with rocks and tight switchbacks (4).

0.3 Go left at a T intersection. This ride loops clockwise and returns to this junction from the right. (Ignore the misplaced sign here indicating the South Rim Trail.) The gradient eases up for a while.

1.5 The trail steepens; expect tight radius switchbacks with poor traction (4+).

1.6 Control your speed and be wary of roots, rocks, and deep ruts.

2.2 Turn right onto South Rim Trail.

2.4 Keep your balance on this narrow section—there is quite a drop on the downhill side.

3.2 Go 50 feet past a shack on the right and turn right on Ten Mile House Road. Begin a challenging 1-mile climb.

4.2 Turn right onto singletrack, the northern branch of Pine Trail.

4.5 Turn left, back up the initial descent of this ride. Prepare for some tough climbing.

4.8 Back to the beginning.

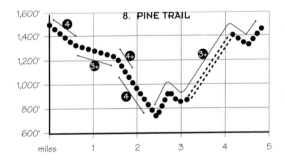

Upper Ponderosa Way

Location: Along the eastern border of the Ishi Wilderness Area, 30 miles (an hour's drive) north of Chico.

Distance: 37.4 miles out and back.

Time: 6 hours.

Tread: 37.4 miles on dirt road.

Aerobic level: Strenuous.

Technical difficulty: Simple when climbing (2); tricky when descending (3+).

Hazards: With high summer temperatures and no drinking fountains, dehydration is in store for the unprepared rider. This ride is not recommended for a solo rider, owing to its fast descents in isolated country.

Highlights: Because the entire ride lies within a state game refuge that borders a designated wilderness area, you have a good chance of seeing wildlife, and are certain to see a large variety of butterflies along the way. The campground at Deer Creek is beautiful and secluded, with a good year-round spring and access to Deer Creek for swimming. Black Rock Mountain is a dramatic geologic anomaly regarded as sacred by Native Americans. This is a challenging ride aerobically with about 5,000 feet of total climbing.

Land status: Lassen National Forest, state game refuge.

Maps: USDA Forest Service Ishi Wilderness pamphlet; USGS 7.5-minute quads for Devils Parade Ground, Barkley Mountain; Lassen National Forest map.

Upper Ponderosa Way

TO (36)
AND RED BLUFF

Black Rock
2,694'

The
Narrows

Mill Creek

27N08

Cedar
Spring

(9)

Flatiron Mtn.
4,400'

Lassen Trail

Ishi Wilderness
Boundary

Moak Trail

Ponderosa Way

Deer Creek

(9)

TO COHASSET
AND CHICO

N

0   2.5   5

MILES

44

Access: From California Highway 99 in Chico, take Cohasset Road north 31 miles through Cohasset to the USDA Forest Service campground on Deer Creek. (At 17.3 miles, Cohasset Road becomes gravel. At about 23 miles, the road becomes dirt—a four-wheel-drive vehicle may be needed during the rainy season.) At a helicopter pad/clearing at 23.9 miles, a large boulder with "Deer Creek" painted on it directs you to continue straight ahead. Ignore the branch to the right at 25 miles; continue straight. Somewhere along the way, this road becomes Ponderosa Way, as noted on most maps but not indicated by any signage. Pass the entrance to Ishi Wilderness at 30.3 miles. This is the trailhead for Deer Creek Trail, a great trail for hiking and fishing but closed to mechanized vehicles (including bikes). Cross Deer Creek on an old bridge at 30.5 miles. Turn right into the campground at 31 miles. Here you will find toilet facilities, a good place to camp, and fine swimming in Deer Creek. The odometer readings start at the information board at the end of the campground road.

The Ride

0.0 This area gets very hot in the summer and a rider can easily drink a gallon of water en route to the year-round spring near Black Rock Mountain—please pack accordingly. Also, as you bomb down these isolated backwoods stretches,

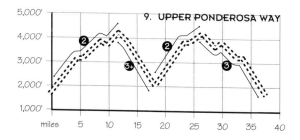

keep in mind the high vulture-to-doctor ratio in this area. To begin, pedal back up the campground road to the main road (Ponderosa Way).

0.2 Turn right on Ponderosa Way, heading north.

0.6 Note the four-wheel-drive road to the right—this drops down to a great camping area with sandy beaches. For now, go straight on Ponderosa Way. In a few more yards stands a tall breccia rock outcropping. There are many of these in this area. They are the result of the differential weathering of volcanic mudflows.

4.4 Road levels off for about 0.7 mile.

5.1 Enjoy a nice outlook to the right. Then it's back to climbing.

7.0 Moak Trailhead to the left. This trail, along with the rest of the Ishi Wilderness, is closed to mechanized vehicles.

8.6 Pass the Lassen Trail where it enters the Ishi Wilderness—return here sometime with your hiking boots on.

13.1 Go left on a dirt road where a sign indicates Black Rock in 5 miles.

17.5 Roll over a short concrete bridge.

17.9 Cross another small concrete bridge.

18.2 Bridge over Mill Creek. The huge rock to the right thrusting upward several hundred feet above Mill Creek is Black Rock Mountain, a sacred site for the Yahi Yana Indians.

18.3 The campground entrance to the left marks your turn-around spot. Pull in here for a quick tour of the campground. The campground road ends at toilets, picnic tables, and a place to ease into the cold waters of Mill Creek. Turn around here and prepare to climb.

18.5 Back across Mill Creek Bridge. Delicious blackberries and a fresh spring can be found on the south side of the bridge.

20.7 Has that huge boulder precariously poised over the road caught your attention?

23.5 Cedar Spring (to the left) is seasonal.

23.6 Take a detour by going left on Ponderosa Way (Forest Road 27N08) toward The Narrows.

23.9 The Narrows. Walk on a short path on ridge for a view of some very intriguing rock formations. To finish the ride, go back to Ponderosa Way and head south toward Deer Creek Campground.

37.2 Turn left onto the campground road.

37.4 Back to your car and a fine place for a cool swim!

Deer Creek Trail

Location: 39 miles north-northeast of Chico, alongside Deer Creek.

Distance: 12.4 miles out and back.

Time: 3 to 5 hours.

Tread: 1 mile on dirt road; 11.4 miles on singletrack.

Aerobic level: Moderate with numerous short, strenuous sections.

Technical difficulty: Varies from 3 to 5+; you may have to dab or dismount as many as 50 times to get through a multitude of very short but steep or rocky sections. This is a very good ride for intermediate through expert riders.

Hazards: Singletrack trail is narrow on steep hillsides in various sections. Poison oak grows along most of the trail. Numerous short rocky sections are fairly easy to walk but very challenging

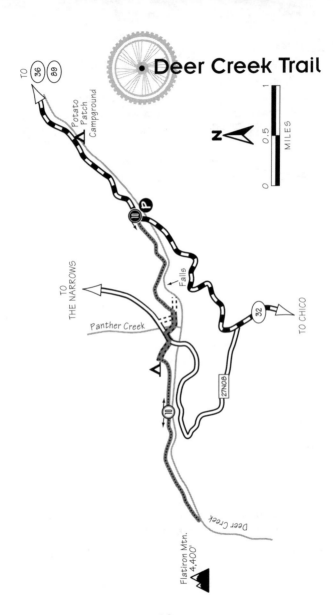

Deer Creek Trail

TO 36 89

Potato Patch Campground

MILES
0 0.5 1

N

TO THE NARROWS

Panther Creek

Falls

P

TO CHICO

32

27N08

Deer Creek

Flatiron Mtn.
4,400'

to ride. Please be careful on this ride—getting medical attention in this rugged country would be difficult.

Highlights: Entire ride is exceptionally beautiful, a hiking trail used long ago by the Yahi Yana Indians, most notably Ishi, the last of his tribe and the last-known man in California to live aboriginally. Anyone who tries this ride is sure to return, if not to mountain bike, then to hike, fish, or swim.

Land status: Lassen National Forest.

Maps: USGS 7.5-minute quads for Onion Butte, Barkley Mountain; Lassen National Forest map.

Access: From California Highway 99 in Chico, drive 39 miles northeast on CA 32, just past the first bridge across Deer Creek, and park in the paved turnout on the right side of the road. (The Potato Patch Forest Service Campground is 1.7 miles farther up CA 32 on the right. This is a fine campground with toilets and an artesian well across the highway from the entrance.)

The Ride

0.0   Pedal back toward the bridge on the north side of the highway to where you first meet the guardrail. Look up the shoulder and you'll see a sign, "Deer Creek Trail." This is the trailhead to the Deer Creek Trail, also known as the

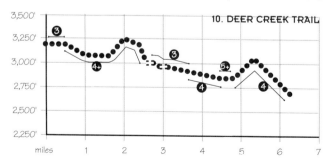

Ishi Trail. Take this singletrack west and begin a long overall descent above and alongside Deer Creek.

0.5 Rocky technical (4+) section.

1.7 More technical stuff—most riders will choose to walk through this.

1.9 Go right at a Y junction.

2.3 Hang on for a very steep descent with tight switchbacks (4+). Please walk here if you cannot negotiate this without skidding your tires. Improper use of this trail by mountain bikers could result in loss of access.

2.4 As the descent bottoms out, turn right onto an unimproved road; head west.

2.6 Take singletrack that branches off to the left. If you miss the singletrack, you soon encounter a gravel road (Forest Road 27N08), which if taken to the left, intercepts the ride at mile 2.8 below.

2.7 Portage a small creek.

2.8 Singletrack ends on a gravel road (FR 27N08). Turn left here and go 50 yards. Before the bridge, turn right onto a dirt road and roll into a campground area.

3.1 About 100 yards before the end of the campground road, take singletrack west, back onto Deer Creek Trail.

3.5 Creek crossing. Caution: the trail becomes narrow and washed out, with loose sand and gravel on a steep hillside.

4.5 Very technical (5+) sections just ahead, which ordinary mortals must hike through.

4.9 Steep, rocky climb. Keep to the right and, if you must fall, fall to the right.

5.2 Walk through a gully. (Don't feel inadequate if you need to walk the many other short sections that aren't mentioned in this text—we're here to have fun, right?)

6.2 The trail drops down to the creek and becomes vague in loose sand. Continue a short distance close to the creek until the tread is too loose to ride and swimming holes are

visible to the left. Notice several very large pine trees—
this is the end of the trail. Take a dip and then retrace
your tracks back to CA 32.

9.4 Back onto a gravel road. Take the singletrack that starts 5
feet past a sign reading "The Narrows—15."

10.5 Lower Deer Creek Falls below.

12.4 Back on CA 32. Wasn't that great?

Colby Mountain Lookout

Location: Lassen National Forest northeast of Butte Meadows,
35 miles north-northeast of Chico.

Distance: 11.9 miles.

Time: 2 hours.

Tread: 1.4 miles on paved road; 10.5 miles on unimproved
road.

Aerobic level: Moderate.

Technical difficulty: Mostly 2 with some fairly short sections
of 3+.

Hazards: The first leg of the descent on the return from the top
of Colby Mountain is riddled with loose rocks, small branches,
and other loose material.

Highlights: Meadow area along Colby Creek is lush with vegetation during the middle of summer. Colby Mountain has a

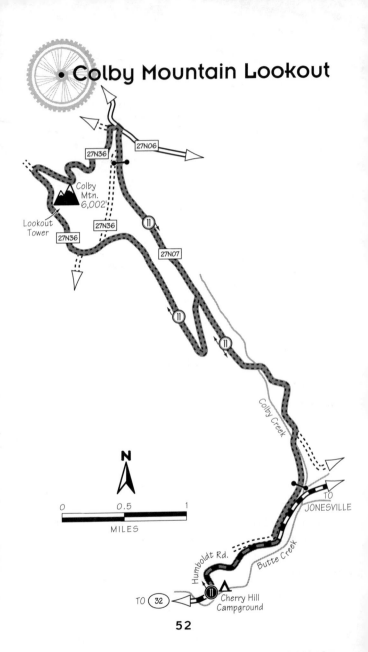

Colby Mountain Lookout

27N36

27N06

Colby
Mtn.
6,002'

Lookout
Tower

27N36

27N36

11

27N07

11

11

Colby Creek

N

TO
JONESVILLE

0   0.5   1

MILES

Humboldt Rd.

Butte Creek

TO 32

11

Cherry Hill
Campground

fire lookout that affords a panoramic view of Lassen National Forest. This ride offers solitude and good odds of seeing wildlife such as bears and deer.

Land status: Lassen National Forest.

Maps: USGS 7.5-minute quads for Jonesville, Humboldt Peak, and Onion Butte; Lassen National Forest map.

Access: From California Highway 99 in Chico, take CA 32 east 27.2 miles. Turn right on Humboldt Road and go 8.8 miles northeast to Cherry Hill Campground. Park here.

The Ride

0.0 From the entrance to Cherry Hill Campground, cycle north up Humboldt Road toward Jonesville alongside Butte Creek.

0.7 Take the dirt road to the left of Humboldt Road and head northeast, paralleling Humboldt Road for the next 0.5 mile.

1.2 Squeeze by an old steel gate.

1.6 Portage Colby Creek. In another 30 yards, notice a large pile of rocks and turn left onto a dirt road, traveling north through a lush meadow along Colby creek.

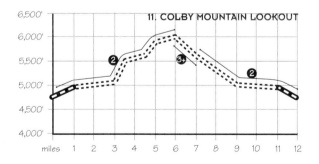

2.1 Go left at the fork.

2.3 Cross Colby Creek again.

3.1 Take a hard left and head south at this double-Y intersection. (The return loop from Colby Mountain connects here from the north.) The road gets a little rougher here and the grade increases.

3.6 The road switches back to the right and begins a serious climb northwest toward Colby Mountain Lookout.

5.0 Turn left onto another dirt road. This is Forest Road 27N36—although it may not be identified at this juncture.

5.8 Colby Mountain Lookout—elevation 6,002 feet. Climb a few stairs and take in a panoramic view which includes Lassen Peak to the north. Continue the ride by cycling past the vehicle turnaround and picking up a narrow dirt road, heading northwest through the chaparral.

6.0 The road (actually more like a doubletrack trail at this point) splits at a pile of rocks. Take a right and head east. (In another 100 yards or so to the west, the trail ends at a nice lookout.) The next mile or so is a serpentine, tricky descent, with lots of small obstacles and loose material (3+).

7.2 The road ends at another dirt road. Take this to the right and go up about 80 yards to a gravel road. Turn right again, heading east. After another 50 yards, another dirt road appears to the right with a sign indicating that this road (FR 27N36) leads to Colby Mountain Lookout. Take this right in a southerly direction. (Don't fret—you won't have to make that tough climb again!)

7.4 Go left at a Y junction.

7.9 Washed-out section of road—careful!

8.7 Keep going south here (remember this intersection?), back onto the section of the ride that comprised the first 3.1 miles.

10.3 Large rockpile to the left; cross Colby Creek to the right.

10.7 Past the old, rusty steel gate again—stay to the right.

11.2 Turn right onto Humboldt Road.

11.9 Welcome back to Cherry Hill Campground.

Humbug Summit

Location: Lassen National Forest east of Butte Meadows, 30 miles north-northeast of Chico.

Distance: 30.2-mile loop.

Time: 3.5 hours.

Tread: 6.6 miles on paved road; 5.2 miles on gravel road; 18.4 miles on unimproved road.

Aerobic level: Moderate.

Technical difficulty: Mostly 2 with sections of 3, depending on seasonal changes.

Hazards: Occasional cars and trucks could be a big problem for maniacal downhillers. Gravel portion of Humboldt Road is quite smooth, but offers little traction.

Highlights: Cherry Hill and Butte Meadows offer inexpensive, creekside campsites and both are close to start/finish of the ride. Most of this ride is in Lassen National Forest, with the upper portion offering solitude and comfortably cool summer temperatures.

Land status: Lassen National Forest and public roads.

Humbug Summit

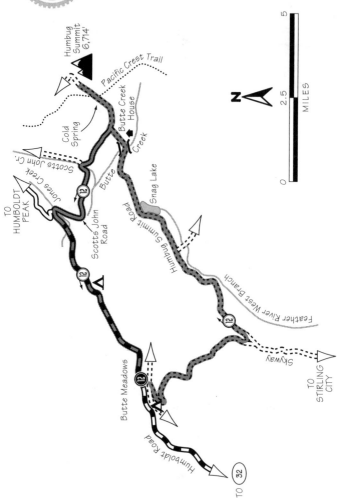

56

Maps: USGS 7.5-minute quads for Butte Meadows, Jonesville; Lassen National Forest map.

Access: From California Highway 99 in Chico, take CA 32 east 27.2 miles. Turn right on Humboldt Road and go northeast 5.3 miles. Stop at the intersection of Humboldt Road and Skyway and park nearby. (Butte Meadows Campground is back down Humboldt Road 0.3 mile on the south side of the road. Cherry Hill Campground is 3.5 miles farther up Humboldt Road.)

The Ride

0.0   Starting at the intersection of Humboldt Road and Sky-way, pedal south down Skyway. The road changes from pavement to dirt after about 0.3 mile.
0.5   Stay left at a Y—take the high road.
5.9   A sign at a fork in the road indicates Stirling City to the right, Lake Almanor to the left. Go left, toward Lake Almanor.
6.0   Skyway merges onto Humbug Summit Road. Bear left, heading northeast. Enjoy a fast, 0.8-mile descent—watch your speed!
8.5   Nice view of the Feather River West Branch.

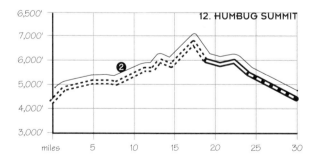

10.1 Keep on the road to the left.

11.5 Snag Lake on the right

14.4 Bridge crosses Butte Creek. Historic Butte Creek House to the right.

15.2 Notice the road to your left—you'll be taking this on your way back down from the summit. The forest becomes predominantly Douglas-fir covered with moss.

16.5 Humbug Summit Road crosses the Pacific Crest Trail (which is closed to mechanized vehicles). Walk up the trail about 10 feet and look to the west about 50 yards. Cold Spring is an artesian spring piped to conveniently provide pure, cold water.

17.0 Humbug Summit—elevation 6,714 feet! Turn around and speed down 1.8 miles, unsuspecting of old folks towing really big trailers head-on smack down the middle of the road.

18.8 Turn right onto a gravel road (informally known as Scotts John Road), heading northeast toward Humboldt Road, along Scotts John Creek. For the next 2 miles you may enjoy rapid acceleration, experimenting with two-wheel drift on loose gravel.

20.6 Stay left and cross Scotts John Creek.

23.8 Merge left onto Humboldt Road. The road soon becomes paved and winds through the quiet little town of Jonesville. (See Ride 10 for more climbing from this point.)

25.6 Humboldt Road crosses Jones Creek.

26.7 Cherry Hill Campground to the left.

29.0 Beautiful meadow on the left.

30.2 Back to the intersection of Skyway and Humboldt Road.

Humboldt Summit

Location: Lassen National Forest east of Butte Meadows, 35 miles north-northeast of Chico.

Distance: 14.6 miles out and back.

Time: 2 hours.

Tread: 5.8 miles on paved road; 8.8 miles on unimproved road.

Aerobic level: Moderate.

Technical difficulty: Mostly 2 with sections of 3 depending on seasonal changes.

Hazards: A 1-mile section of Humboldt Road has some sheer drop-offs at the shoulder and sometimes the shoulder is missing.

Highlights: Impressive view of Lassen Peak and intermediate ridges from Humboldt Summit. Most of this ride is in Lassen National Forest, with the upper portion offering solitude and comfortably cool summer temperatures.

Land status: Lassen National Forest and public roads.

Maps: USGS 7.5-minute quads for Jonesville, Humboldt Peak; Lassen National Forest map.

Access: From California Highway 99 in Chico, take CA 32 east 27.2 miles. Turn right on Humboldt Road and go northeast 8.8 miles to Cherry Hill Campground. Park here.

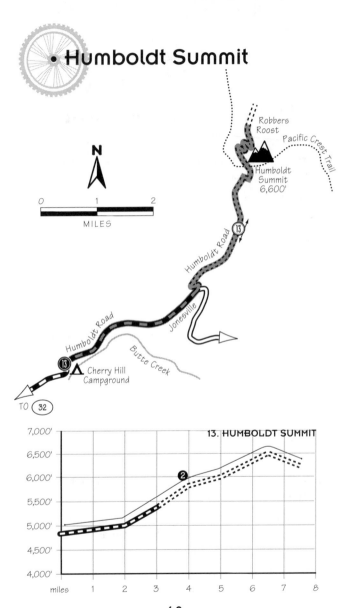

• Humboldt Summit

Robbers Roost

Pacific Crest Trail

Humboldt Summit 6,600'

N

0   1   2

MILES

Humboldt Road

⑬

Jonesville

Humboldt Road

Butte Creek

⑬

Cherry Hill Campground

TO ③②

7,000'
6,500'
6,000'
5,500'
5,000'
4,500'
4,000'

13. HUMBOLDT SUMMIT

❷

miles   1   2   3   4   5   6   7   8

The Ride

0.0 From the entrance to Cherry Hill Campground cycle north up Humboldt Road toward Jonesville along Butte Creek.

2.9 The pavement changes to dirt and gravel at a Y junction. Go left up toward Humboldt Summit.

6.3 Humboldt Road crosses the Pacific Crest Trail (which is closed to mechanized vehicles). This is Humboldt Summit, elevation 6,600 feet. Lassen Peak can be seen to the north. Tired riders may wish to turn around at this point, but everyone else can continue another mile on Humboldt Road to experience a little history. CAUTION: The next mile has some cliffs to the side of the road and sections of road may be washed out.

7.3 Congratulations, you've just passed through Robbers Roost without getting ambushed. Turn around here and head back up toward Humboldt Summit and ponder the logistics of a stagecoach robbery.

8.3 Humboldt Summit again. Continue back down toward Cherry Hill Campground and appreciate a 1,900-foot descent.

14.6 Cherry Hill Campground.

Philbrook Lake to Lotts Lake

Location: In Lassen National Forest, 44 miles northeast of Chico. (Allow 1.25 hours driving time each way.)

Distance: 11.7-mile loop.

Time: About 2 hours.

Tread: 9.3 miles on unimproved road; 1.6 miles on doubletrack; 0.8 mile on singletrack.

Aerobic level: Moderate.

Technical difficulty: Pretty smooth (2+) for most of the ride, with a very short stretch to hike and a little bit of modest singletrack (3+). Return leg is a little more challenging (3+) than ride out.

Hazards: Cyclists must share this ride with a variety of off-highway vehicles, especially on weekends. Fast descents could get a rider in trouble on loose dirt and gravel roads.

Highlights: Philbrook Lake is a pleasant family campground and provides good access to the High Lakes area (see Ride 15). Ride is a moderate climb to a beautiful natural lake and a fast, fun return.

Land status: Lassen National Forest, public roads, and private land.

Maps: U.S. Forest Service pamphlet, "Off-Highway Vehicle Trails of the Almanor Ranger District"; USGS 7.5-minute quad for Jonesville; Lassen National Forest map.

Philbrook Lake to Lotts Lake

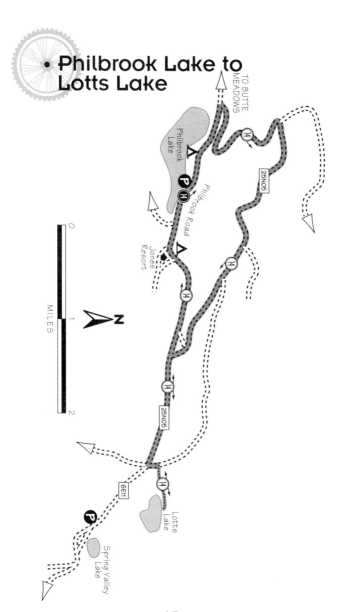

TO BUTTE MEADOWS

Philbrook Lake

Philbrook Road

Jones Resort

25N05

Lotts Lake

Spring Valley Lake

6E11

N

MILES

0   1   2

Access: From California Highway 99 in Chico, take CA 32 east 27.2 miles. Turn right on Humboldt Road and go northeast 5.3 miles. Turn right onto Skyway; go another 6.1 miles and bear left at a Y junction. In another 0.1 mile turn left onto Humbug Summit Road. Continue 1.7 miles and turn right on Philbrook Road. Go 3.2 miles and keep right at a fork. Drive another 1.1 miles and park in the Philbrook Lake day-use area. (Campsites are usually available during the week back in the main area. Free campsites are located up ahead on the left just before Jones Resort. Jones Resort has everything from tent campsites to cabins.)

The Ride

0.0 From the Philbrook Lake day-use area, pedal west, back toward Butte Meadows.

1.1 Turn hard right on Forest Road 25N05.

5.0 Keep right at a fork in the road.

6.1 The road cuts though rock stratum.

6.2 Notice a four-wheel-drive road joining in from the west—you'll be returning on it. Look up to the left for cleverly painted rock.

7.4 This road ends at another dirt road. Turn left, go 20 yards, then turn right onto yet another dirt road, heading east again.

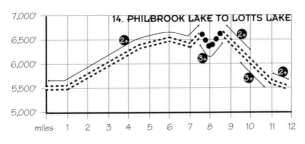

7.5 The four-wheel-drive road ends and a singletrack/hiking trail picks up here after a barrier of fallen trees. Lotts Lake can be seen below, to the east. Take this singletrack about 50 yards, then portage down a steep slope another 50 yards. Continue cycling east as the trail levels off.

7.8 Pass a large granite formation on the right and follow narrow singletrack a few yards farther until it approaches Lotts Lake.

7.9 Stop where the trail comes down a few feet away from the lake and enjoy the view. (The north end of the lake lies in Lassen National Forest; the remainder resides in a small patch of private land.) Turn around here and retrace your tracks for the next 1.7 miles.

9.6 Turn left onto a four-wheel-drive road.

9.7 Ride past a berm and continue down the four-wheel-drive road. This area is private and has been closed to motorized vehicles. Please be especially considerate here so that the road will remain open to mountain bikers.

9.8 Turn left onto another four-wheel-drive road, heading west.

10.2 Turn off the road at a tree marked with a national forest boundary sign, and catch a vague doubletrack trail by heading northwest. The tree and trail are immediately after a small rock drainage that crosses the road, but just before a clearing. Don't worry if you aren't sure of the trail. Just keep on a due-west heading and the trail will become more obvious.

10.6 The trail drops fast over the next 0.4 mile.

11.0 The trail ends at Jones Resort driveway. Turn right here. (Jones Resort sells snacks and cold drinks.) Follow the driveway past Jones Resort and turn right onto the road that leads back to the Philbrook Lake day-use area.

11.7 Back at your car.

Spring Valley Lake to Ben Lomond

Location: In Lassen National Forest, a 50-mile drive northeast of Chico. (Allow 1.5 hours driving time each way.)

Distance: 15.5 miles out and back.

Time: 3 to 4.5 hours.

Tread: 15.5 miles on unimproved four-wheel-drive road.

Aerobic level: Strenuous.

Technical difficulty: Very challenging without being too scary; ride averages about -4 with lots of fairly tough sections (-4 to 5).

Hazards: Lots of roots, rocks, and slippery sections could send you head over heels if you are overzealous on the downhills. This is a very rugged, remote area. Bring snacks, plenty of water, and at least one other rider for safety.

Highlights: The High Lakes area is a pristine, rugged forest full of streams, natural lakes, and beautiful views. Due to its average elevation of about 6,000 feet, it is usually about 20 degrees cooler than Chico and makes for some very comfortable summer riding. (This area is snowbound during the colder months; check with the USDA Forest Service or call Philbrook Resort for local conditions.)

Land status: Lassen National Forest.

Maps: USDA Forest Service pamphlet, "Off-Highway Vehicle Trails of the Almanor Ranger District"; USGS 7.5-minute quads

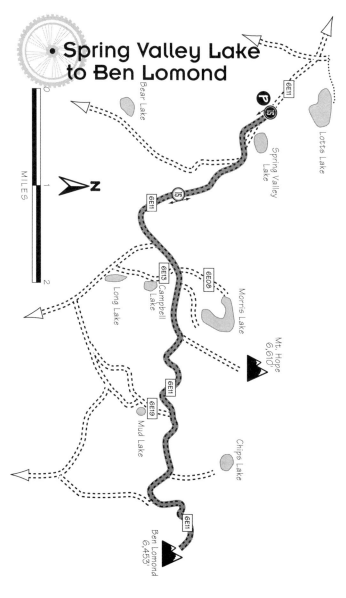

Spring Valley Lake to Ben Lomond

MILES

Z

Bear Lake

Lotts Lake

Spring Valley Lake

6E11

P 15

15

6E11

Long Lake

6E13

Campbell Lake

6E08

Morris Lake

Mt. Hope 6,610'

6E11

6E19

Mud Lake

Chips Lake

6E11

Ben Lomond 6,453'

for Jonesville, Belden, Kimshew Point, Storrie; Lassen National Forest map.

Access: From California Highway 99 in Chico, take CA 32 east 27.2 miles. Turn right on Humboldt Road and go northeast 5.3 miles. Turn right onto Skyway, go another 6.1 miles, and bear left at a Y junction. In 0.1 mile turn left onto Humbug Summit Road. Continue another 1.7 miles and turn right on Philbrook Road. Go another 3.2 miles and turn left at a Y onto Forest Road 25N05. Go 4 miles and keep right at another Y. Drive 2.4 miles until the road ends at an unmarked dirt road. (If you are driving a small car with low clearance or poor traction, consider parking here and incorporating the next 0.9 mile into the bike ride—the road ahead is very rough.) Turn right here, continue 100 yards, and bear left at a Y. Go another 0.6 mile and pass through the entrance to the USDA Forest Service designated Off-Highway Vehicle (OHV) area. Go 0.2 mile farther and park in the parking area to the right.

The Ride

0.0 From the parking area just above Spring Valley Lake, pedal down the four-wheel-drive road toward the lake.

0.1 Go right at a Y junction. Slow for a washed-out rocky section just ahead (5).

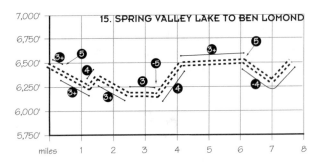

0.3 Cross a small stream just before the road approaches Spring Valley Lake.

0.6 Go right at another Y. In 50 yards, keep going straight where another track branches right to Bear Lake.

1.2 Gear down for a moderate technical (4) climb over the next 0.2 mile.

1.8 Granite cliffs rise to the left, then the track skirts a meadow.

2.1 The washed-out section ahead features fixed rocks as well as loose gravel and cobbles.

2.6 Go left at a Y junction; stay on FR 6E11.

2.8 Stream crossing. The road becomes smoother and level.

2.9 FR 6E13 branches right to Campbell Lake; continue straight.

3.0 FR 6E08 branches left to Morris Lake. Keep going straight on a northeast heading.

3.2 Continue straight, past a road branching left. The tread becomes strenuous and rocky (-5).

3.3 Enjoy a beautiful view to the south, overlooking Campbell Lake and Long Lake. The tread mellows out (3+).

3.6 Keep going straight (past a road branching left), heading east-northeast.

3.7 Go right at a fork, heading east toward a granite ridge. Steel yourself for a strenuous technical (4) climb ahead.

4.2 FR 6E19 goes right to Mud Lake. Continue straight, heading east.

5.0 Stay on FR 6E11. A short, tough climb is just ahead.

5.1 A road branches left to Chips Lake; keep to the right. The trail levels off briefly, then begins another steep climb.

5.3 Roll onto the ridgetop with a scenic view to the east.

5.9 Pass through a mellow section with a canyon to the left and meadow to the right. The tread is a mosaic pattern of flat igneous rock.

6.2	The trail drops quickly; watch out for a short rocky section (5), where the trail branches and braids back together.
7.0	The trail levels off and leaves the forest canopy.
7.1	Another steep climb.
7.5	Enjoy a panoramic view from the northwest around to the south.
7.7	The trail ends at Ben Lomond, a peak overlooking the North Fork of the Feather River 4,000 feet below! Turn around here and reverse your route to return to the start.
15.5	Back at your automobile.

(West) Bullards Bar Trail

Location: New Bullards Bar Reservoir, 65 miles southeast of Chico.

Distance: 11.2 miles out and back.

Time: 1.5 hours.

Tread: 1 mile on unimproved road; 10.2 miles on singletrack.

Aerobic level: Easy.

Technical difficulty: Well-maintained singletrack consistently averages about -3.

(West) Bullards Bar Trail

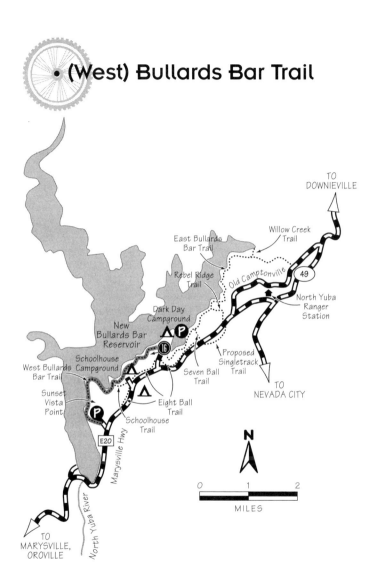

TO
DOWNIEVILLE

Willow Creek
Trail

East Bullards
Bar Trail

Old Camptonville

49

Rebel Ridge
Trail

North Yuba
Ranger
Station

Dark Day
Campground

New
Bullards Bar
Reservoir

16

Schoolhouse
Campground

Proposed
Singletrack
Trail

West Bullards
Bar Trail

Seven Ball
Trail

TO
NEVADA CITY

Sunset
Vista
Point

P

Eight Ball
Trail

E20

Schoolhouse
Trail

Marysville Hwy

N

0   1   2

MILES

TO
MARYSVILLE,
OROVILLE

North Yuba River

Hazards: Some fairly steep drops on the downhill side of the singletrack requiring reasonable speeds. Loose leaves and pine needles can be slippery.

Highlights: A very smooth, gently rising and dropping, curvy singletrack trail close to the reservoir, with lots of shade, providing a fun and scenic ride. New Bullards Bar Reservoir offers opportunities for boating, fishing, camping, and swimming. Call 530-692-3200 for campsite reservations.

Land status: Tahoe National Forest.

Maps: USGS 7.5-minute quads for Challenge, Camptonville; Plumas National Forest map; USDA Forest Service Bullards Bar brochure.

Access: From the intersection of California Highway 32 and CA 99 in Chico, drive 10.7 miles south on CA 99. Turn left onto CA 149, heading east another 4.7 miles. Turn right on CA 70 and go south 6.4 miles. Take the CA 162 exit (Richvale Oro Dam Road), and turn left at the stop light, heading east. Drive 7.4 miles on CA 162 (bearing right at 2 miles), then turn right on Miner's Ranch/Wyandotte Road. Go another 2.6 miles and then turn left on Oro Bangor Highway (which becomes Verjeles Road up ahead). Travel another 11.8 miles and turn left on Loma Rica Road. Continue 1.4 miles and turn left on County Road E21 (Marysville Road). Go another 2.6 miles and turn

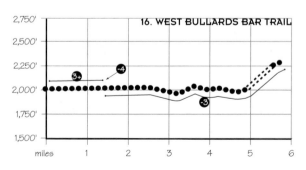

right on CR E20 (still Marysville Road). Drive 17.3 miles and turn left into Dark Day picnic and camping area. Go down this paved entrance road 0.5 mile and turn left at a Y junction. Another 0.4 mile puts you in the Dark Day picnic parking area. The ride begins here.

The Ride

0.0 Catch the singletrack 50 feet southwest of the parking area. The trailhead sign is marked "West Bullards Trail 8E07."

0.8 Turn right at a T intersection onto a road with old, unmaintained pavement.

0.9 Turn left onto singletrack.

2.5 Continue straight, past Schoolhouse Trail, toward Vista Point.

2.9 Ride through a pleasant stream crossing.

3.0 Another cool stream crossing.

3.1 Go straight ahead, past an abandoned trail.

5.0 Turn left onto an unimproved road; start climbing.

5.5 Bear right onto singletrack.

5.6 Sunset Vista Point parking area. Drinking water and toilets are available here. Turn around and retrace your route.

11.2 Back at Dark Day picnic parking area.

(East) Bullards Bar Trail

Location: New Bullards Bar Reservoir, 65 miles southeast of Chico.

Distance: 16.8 miles out and back.

Time: 2.5 to 3 hours.

Tread: 16.8 miles on singletrack! The upper 3-mile section is an old service road converted to a hiking, equestrian, and biking trail.

Aerobic level: Moderate.

Technical difficulty: Ride averages about 3+; you must have a good sense of balance for narrow sections of singletrack.

Hazards: Occasional poison oak; sections with loose leaves and pine needles; off-camber turns; unexpected quick turns; narrow sections sloping outward toward fairly steep drops.

Highlights: This is one of the longest and best singletrack rides in this book. The trail is well maintained. Upper portion is wide, smooth, fast, and fun. Trail is almost entirely shaded and pretty. New Bullards Bar Reservoir offers opportunities for boating, fishing, camping, and swimming. (Call 530-692-3200 for campsite reservations.)

Land status: Tahoe National Forest.

Maps: USGS 7.5-minute quads for Challenge, Camptonville; Plumas National Forest map.

(East) Bullards Bar Trail

Willow Creek Trail

East Bullards Bar Trail

Rebel Ridge Trail

Old Camptonville

17

49

TO DOWNIEVILLE

North Yuba Ranger Station

Dark Day Campground

New Bullards Bar Reservoir

17

Proposed Singletrack Trail

Schoolhouse Campground

West Bullards Bar Trail

Seven Ball Trail

TO NEVADA CITY

Sunset Vista Point

P

Eight Ball Trail

Schoolhouse Trail

E20

Marysville Hwy

North Yuba River

N

0   1   2
MILES

TO MARYSVILLE, OROVILLE

Access: From the intersection of California Highway 32 and CA 99 in Chico, drive 10.7 miles south on CA 99. Turn left onto CA 149, heading east another 4.7 miles. Turn right on CA 70 and go south 6.4 miles. Take the CA 162 exit (Richvale Oro Dam Road), and turn left at the stop light, heading east. Drive 7.4 miles on CA 162 (bearing right at 2 miles), then turn right on Miner's Ranch/Wyandotte Road. Go another 2.6 miles and then turn left on Oro Bangor Highway (which becomes Verjeles Road up ahead). Travel another 11.8 miles and turn left on Loma Rica Road. Continue 1.4 miles and turn left on County Road E21 (Marysville Road). Go another 2.6 miles and turn right on CR E20 (still Marysville Road). Drive 17.3 miles and turn left into Dark Day picnic and camping area. Go down this paved entrance road 0.5 mile and turn left at a Y junction. Another 0.4 mile puts you in the Dark Day picnic parking area. The ride begins here.

The Ride

0.0 Start pedaling east from the Dark Day picnic parking area, back up the paved entrance road about 50 yards. Turn left onto singletrack by the restrooms.

0.1 Pedal east, directly across Dark Day boat parking lot, toward a trailhead sign for Bullards Bar Trail 8E07.

0.2 Catch singletrack on the east side of the boat parking lot.

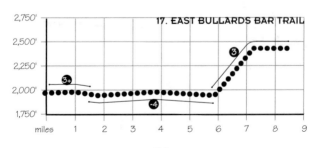

0.8 Small stream crossing; be careful and stay centered on the trail when negotiating a short metal ramp here.

1.4 The trail narrows; it's a steep drop to the left (-4).

1.7 Continue straight, past Seven Ball Trail, toward CA 49.

5.8 The trail becomes considerably wider, smoother, and straighter. Prepare for a steady climb, gaining about 600 feet in elevation.

6.5 Bear right, past Willow Creek Trail, toward CA 49. (The signed mileage for CA 49 is wrong.)

8.3 Cross a jeep trail, continuing east.

8.4 Old Camptonville Road (paved). Catch your breath. Turn around and enjoy a very nice descent.

16.8 Back to Dark Day picnic parking area.

Eight Ball Trail

Location: New Bullards Bar Reservoir, 65 miles southeast of Chico.

Distance: 15.8-mile loop.

Time: 1.5 to 2.5 hours.

Tread: 2.3 miles on paved road; 0.5 mile on unimproved road; 13 miles on singletrack.

Aerobic level: Moderate, with one moderately strenuous climb.

Technical difficulty: Averages about 3+.

Hazards: Occasional poison oak; sections with loose leaves

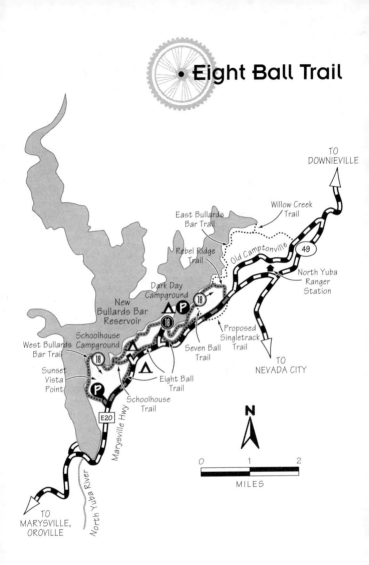

Eight Ball Trail

TO DOWNIEVILLE

Willow Creek Trail

East Bullards Bar Trail

Rebel Ridge Trail

Old Camptonville

49

North Yuba Ranger Station

Dark Day Campground

New Bullards Bar Reservoir

18

18

Schoolhouse Campground

West Bullards Bar Trail

18

Seven Ball Trail

Proposed Singletrack Trail

TO NEVADA CITY

Sunset Vista Point

P

Eight Ball Trail

E20

Schoolhouse Trail

Marysville Hwy

N

0   1   2
MILES

North Yuba River

TO MARYSVILLE, OROVILLE

and pine needles; ruts and loose pine cones; off-camber turns; unexpected quick turns; narrow sections sloping outward toward fairly steep drops.

Highlights: This ride is a great introduction to most of the trails around New Bullards Bar Reservoir. It includes Eight Ball Trail, Rebel Ridge Trail, and the easier portions of Bullards Trail. Most of the ride is smooth singletrack under forest canopy. Drinking water and toilets are available at several spots along the way. The ride begins and ends at a picnic area with access to the reservoir for swimming. New Bullards Bar Reservoir also offers opportunities for boating, fishing, and camping. (Call 530-692-3200 for campsite reservations.)

Land status: Tahoe National Forest.

Maps: USGS 7.5-minute quads for Challenge, Camptonville; Plumas National Forest map.

Access: From the intersection of California Highway 32 and CA 99 in Chico, drive 10.7 miles south on CA 99. Turn left onto CA 149, heading east another 4.7 miles. Turn right on CA 70 and go south 6.4 miles. Take the CA 162 exit (Richvale Oro Dam Road), and turn left at the stop light, heading east. Drive 7.4 miles on CA 162 (bearing right at 2 miles), then turn right on Miner's Ranch/Wyandotte Road. Go another 2.6 miles and then turn left on Oro Bangor Highway (which becomes Verjeles Road up ahead). Travel another 11.8 miles and turn left on Loma Rica Road. Continue 1.4 miles and turn left on County Road E21 (Marysville Road). Go another 2.6 miles and turn right on CR E20 (still Marysville Road). Drive 17.3 miles and turn left into Dark Day picnic and camping area. Go down this paved entrance road 0.5 mile and turn left at a Y junction. Another 0.4 mile puts you in the Dark Day picnic parking area. The ride begins here.

The Ride

0.0 Start pedaling east from the Dark Day picnic area parking lot, back up the paved entrance road. In about 50 yards turn left onto singletrack by the restrooms.

0.1 Pedal east, directly across the Dark Day boat parking lot, toward a trailhead sign for Bullards Bar Trail 8E07.

0.2 Catch singletrack on the east side of the boat parking lot.

0.8 Small stream crossing; be careful and stay centered on the trail when negotiating a short metal ramp.

1.4 The trail narrows; watch for a steep drop to the left (-4).

1.7 Continue straight, past Seven Ball Trail, toward CA 49.

3.8 Turn right onto Rebel Ridge Trail and begin a tough climb with numerous switchbacks.

5.2 Come to a clearing at the top of the climb. Turn right onto doubletrack, which soon narrows to singletrack.

5.3 Turn right on an unimproved road.

5.4 After passing a spur going right, turn right where the main road ends at another road. Head south 100 yards up to paved Marysville Road.

5.5 Turn right on Marysville Road.

6.3 Turn right onto a paved road signed for the Bullards Bar Trail.

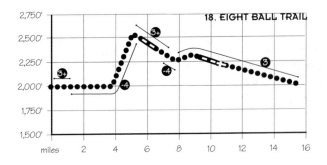

6.4	The top of Seven Ball Trail goes right (and connects to Bullards Bar Trail). Stay straight.
6.6	Go right on singletrack, opposite dump-truck piles of dirt and gravel.
7.2	Hang on for a steep descent ahead with loose tread and quick turns (-4).
7.9	Ride across a paved road (the access road for Dark Day area), and pick up singletrack on the other side.
8.5	The trail widens and skirts campsites, running near the restrooms and a water faucet.
8.6	Go through a dirt clearing with large concrete blocks. (The Schoolhouse Trailhead is just across the paved road here.) Turn left on the paved Schoolhouse Campground access road and ride up to a stop sign.
8.7	Turn right onto singletrack, just before the stop sign.
9.2	Turn right on Marysville Road.
10.1	Turn right onto Sunset Vista Point access road.
10.2	Pick up singletrack just past the restrooms on the left at a sign that reads "Dark Day 5 1/2 miles."
10.3	Go left onto an old paved road.
10.8	Turn right onto singletrack.
12.6	Take singletrack to the left.
13.2	Bear left at a Y junction.
14.8	Merge onto doubletrack, bearing to the right.
14.9	Turn left onto singletrack. Go up 30 yards and bear right at another Y.
15.8	Back to Dark Day picnic area parking.

Feather Falls Loop

Location: 48 miles northeast of Chico.

Distance: 7.7-mile loop.

Time: 1.5 to 2 hours.

Tread: 7.7 miles on singletrack.

Aerobic level: Moderate.

Technical difficulty: Averages about 3.

Hazards: Poison oak and steep drops alongside the trail. Lots of hikers and bikers to share the trails with on weekends.

Highlights: Midpoint of the ride is the overlook for Feather Falls, sixth longest waterfall in the country at 640 feet. More than 7 miles of smooth, well-maintained singletrack with lots of shade in a beautiful forest makes this a pleasurable ride.

Land status: Plumas National Forest.

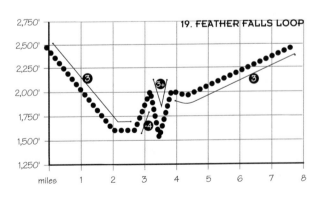

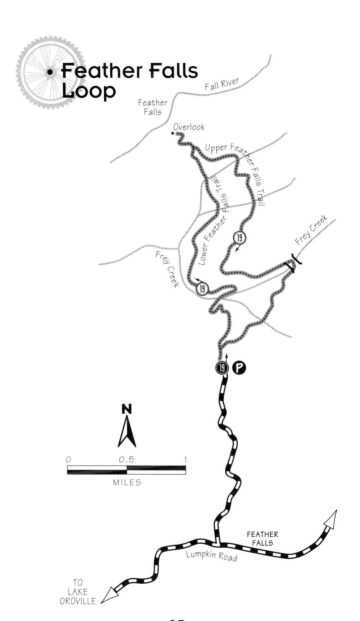

Feather Falls
Loop

Fall River

Feather
Falls

Overlook

Upper Feather Falls Trail

Lower Feather Falls Trail

Frey Creek

19

19

Frey Creek

19 P

N

0   0.5   1

MILES

FEATHER
FALLS

Lumpkin Road

TO
LAKE
OROVILLE

83

Maps: USGS 7.5-minute quads for Forbestown, Brush Creek; Plumas National Forest map.

Access: From the intersection of California Highway 32 and CA 99 in Chico, drive 10.7 miles south on CA 99. Turn left onto CA 149, heading east another 4.7 miles. Turn right on CA 70 and go south 6.4 miles. Take the CA 162 exit (Richvale Oro Dam Road) and turn left at the stop light, heading east. Continue 8.1 miles (get in the right lane at 2 miles) and turn right on Forbestown Road. Go 6.1 miles and turn left on Lumpkin Road. Drive 11 miles, then turn left and drive 0.7 mile into a parking area. Park here and hide any valuables. The ride starts in north end of parking lot, near restrooms and a water faucet.

The Ride

0.0 Start pedaling north on singletrack that begins by the information board.

0.3 Go left at a Y junction, onto the lower trail. Begin the more quickly descending leg of this loop and watch out for roots, rocks, and loose pine needles.

0.4 Very short section of braided trail.

0.8 Watch out for a switchback to the right; the trail's left edge drops off sharply.

1.1 The footbridge over Frey Creek has been washed out; you must wade through this fairly shallow creek.

2.8 Begin a rocky climb.

3.0 Go straight ahead at a junction. (The right branch is the upper trail, the recommended return route.) Get ready for steep climbing ahead; ride or walk as needed.

3.4 Feather Falls Overlook. Relax and enjoy the view before your return climb of 1,200 feet.

3.8 Go left onto the upper trail.

5.6 Bald Rock Dome outlook.

6.3   Cross Frey Creek on a wooden bridge.
7.4   Back onto main trail.
7.7   Parking lot!

Freeman Trail

Location: On the western side of Lake Oroville, 31 miles southeast of Chico.

Distance: 9.3 miles out and back.

Time: 1 to 2 hours.

Tread: 1.3 miles on paved road; 0.4 mile on unimproved road; 7.6 miles on singletrack.

Aerobic level: Moderate overall, although the climb back up the racecourse tends to be more strenuous.

Technical difficulty: Mostly 3+ with a few short, steep, somewhat rocky sections of 4 or 4+.

Hazards: Let's face it—any ride that includes a championship downhill racecourse invites the possibility of manic misfortune. However, the ride is fairly safe for any rider with modest technical skills and a proper regard for gravity.

Highlights: The radical singletrack descent at the beginning of this ride is the racecourse for the California State Championship Downhill Mountain Bike Race! Once you've had your thrill, you can settle down to a fair pace on a smooth, well-groomed singletrack that winds through oak-studded grassy

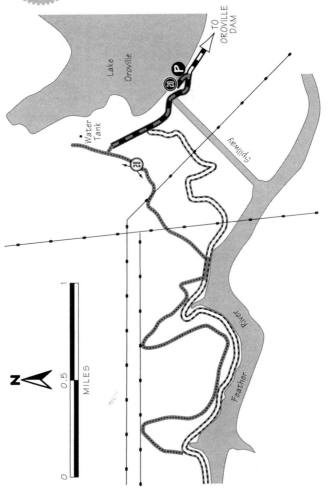

Freeman Trail

Lake Oroville

Water Tank

Spillway

Feather River

TO OROVILLE DAM

N

MILES

0   0.5   1

hills overlooking the very scenic Feather River (Thermalito Diversion Pool). Also, if you time it right, you may enjoy a beautiful sunset when you get back to the parking lot.

Land status: California State Recreation Area; private.

Maps: USGS 7.5-minute quads for Oroville Dam, Oroville; Bradford B. Freeman Bike Trail map/brochure, available at Greenline Cycles in Oroville.

Access: From the intersection of California Highway 32 and CA 99 in Chico, drive 10.7 miles south on CA 99. Turn left onto CA 149, heading east another 4.7 miles. Turn right on CA 70 and go south 6.4 miles. Take the CA 162 exit (Richvale Oro Dam Road) and turn left at the stop light, heading east. (Greenline Cycles is 1 mile ahead on the right.) Continue another 2 miles and get in the left lane, where maintaining an eastern heading puts you onto Oro Dam Boulevard (County Road B2). Oro Dam Boulevard becomes East Oro Dam Road where it bends to the right. Go another 5.7 miles until you reach Canyon Drive; turn left on Canyon Drive, heading north. Go another 0.5 mile, turn left onto an unnamed road atop Oroville Dam and drive northwest 0.9 mile across dam. Bear right at a fork where a sign offers the choice between a boat launch area and general parking. Go 0.1 mile to road's end, make a U-turn, and park.

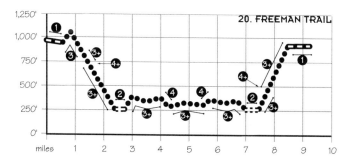

The Ride

0.0   Cycle south to the stop sign at the end of the parking lot and make a U-turn, heading down across the spillway.

0.6   Take the singletrack on the left side at the end of the paved road. Ride down about 50 feet and then take a sharp U-turn to the right, heading uphill to the northeast. Watch out for hardcore downhill maniacs.

0.9   Singletrack meets an unimproved road with a water tank to the right. Notice the picnic table across the road—that is the staging area for the California State Championship National Downhill Mountain Bike Race. Turn around and head back down the singletrack. Take it easy the first time down this exciting racecourse.

1.1   Glide past the singletrack entrance as you begin the steeper part of this descent.

1.6   Steeper, with tighter turns and a few rocks (4+)!

1.7   Grade eases a little (3+).

2.3   End of racecourse. Turn right onto an unimproved road, heading west.

2.5   The road is cut off by an intermittent stream that drains into the Feather River. Take the singletrack to the right. Pedal another 100 feet, cross the stream, and begin a short climb.

2.6   Go right at a Y junction, heading west.

3.3   Part of an old wooden and wire fence here, where the trail branches and braids back together.

3.7   Pass near the corner of a wire fence.

3.9   Go left at a Y, on the lower side.

4.0   The trail descends more steeply and gets rockier (4).

4.1   The trail becomes smooth (3+).

4.8   Singletrack ends at an unimproved road. Turn around here and head back up singletrack. (The unimproved road parallels the river and offers a scenic, easier return back to Oroville Dam.)

7.2 Roll back onto the gravel road for a short breather.

7.4 Take the singletrack (racecourse) on the left back up to the paved road. Now you will earn the potential energy that you spent. Watch out for crazy downhillers.

8.6 Turn right onto a paved road and zip down toward the spillway.

9.0 Pause at the spillway; peer down into the gates on the left and appreciate just how much water is being held at bay.

9.3 Back at the parking lot.

Camp Creek Road

Location: 53.4 miles northwest of Chico.

Distance: 23.6 miles out and back.

Time: 3 to 4 hours.

Tread: 0.2 mile on paved road; 23.4 miles on unimproved road.

Aerobic level: Moderate; see variation to avoid the most difficult climb.

Technical difficulty: Generally 3+ with a couple of slightly rougher sections.

Hazards: Camp Creek Road is a fire and powerline access road and is not maintained to public road standards. Watch for pockets of sand, rocks, and gullies.

Camp Creek Road

TO
QUINCY

Rock Creek

Sugarloaf
Mountain

Camp Creek Road
(Pulga Road)

21

Camp Creek

Camp Creek Road
(Pulga Road)

P

Poe Dam

Pulga

21

P

North Fork Feather River

N

0   1   2

MILES

70

TO
OROVILLE

Highlights: Ride is in the scenic Feather River Canyon and includes dramatic granite outcroppings, numerous waterfalls, and a wide variety of trees, shrubs, and wildflowers.

Land status: Plumas National Forest.

Maps: USGS 7.5-minute quads for Pulga, Kimshew Point, and Storrie; Plumas National Forest map.

Access: From California Highway 32 and CA 99 in Chico, drive 8.2 miles south on CA 99 and exit at Durham-Pentz Road (Butte College exit). Turn left onto Durham-Pentz Road, head east 9.2 miles, and turn right on Pentz Road. Drive 0.5 mile and turn left on CA 70 toward Quincy. Drive 14.7 miles and turn left onto Pulga Road, just before CA 70 crosses the North Fork Feather River. Drive 1 mile and park in the gravel parking area by the railroad tracks. There are no restrooms available on this ride.

The Ride

0.0 Pedal back up Pulga Road. (Artesian spring water can be drawn from the hydrants and hose bibbs on the left side of this first stretch, compliments of Mystic Valley Retreat.)

0.1 Turn right onto Camp Creek Road and start on a steady grind up this rocky road. (Some maps show this as Pulga Road.)

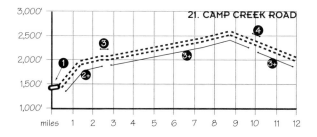

1.4 Pass by a parking area for the variation below, near an intermittent stream.

2.3 Small bridge, stream crossing.

2.6 Fast descent ahead. Watch out for thick patches of sand, rocks, and hungry ruts.

3.2 Wooden bridge crosses a stream with a small waterfall.

3.6 Six-way intersection here. (Now, aren't you glad you have a guidebook?) Go straight, toward the telephone pole 50 yards ahead—just to the right of the road with the "County Road" sign.

5.3 Waterfall, stream crossing.

5.9 Another small waterfall, stream crossing.

6.7 The road splits. Stay right, on the lower side.

7.3 Wooden bridge, waterfall. CAUTION: Slots between planking can trap tires; play it safe by riding along center portion of bridge.

8.5 Small waterfall, stream crossing.

8.8 This is the apex of the ride.

9.8 Wooden bridge, waterfall. CAUTION: Large ruts (gullies) may be lying in wait for some hapless cyclist in the next 0.5 mile or so.

11.8 Nice view of CA 70 crossing Feather River North Fork, as well as Rock Creek and the railroad tracks used to transport spent nuclear fuel from China! Road ends in another 50 yards where a hiking trail begins at a stream crossing. Turn around here and head back to Pulga. (Riders may wish to stash their bikes and hike up about 0.5 mile for a dramatic view of Rock Creek.)

23.6 Back at the parking area. Hike a short distance along the creek and go for a plunge in the Feather River.

Variation: To shave off 2.8 miles and 500 feet of climbing, drive to mile 1.4 in the description above and park on Camp Creek Road.

Upper Miocene Canal

Location: 22 miles east of Chico, just east of Paradise.

Distance: 10.1 miles out and back.

Time: 1.5 to 2.5 hours.

Tread: 0.4 mile on gravel road; 6.1 miles on singletrack.

Aerobic level: Easy.

Technical difficulty: Mostly 3.

Hazards: Narrow walkways atop numerous raised flumes require dismounting. Although no real technical riding is required, a good sense of balance is needed to walk safely over flumes. Any rider foolish enough to attempt to bicycle across flume walkways will graciously delete himself or herself from the gene pool. Several short sections of narrow and out-sloped trail with a steep shoulder (3+) require careful riding.

Highlights: A pleasant, cool ride along Upper Miocene Canal, overlooking the West Branch of the Feather River. An easy ride with a wide variety of trees, shrubs, birds, and wildflowers.

Land status: Pacific Gas and Electric Company.

Maps: USGS 7.5-minute quads for Cherokee, Paradise East.

Access: From California Highway 32 and CA 99 in Chico, drive 8.2 miles south on CA 99 and exit at Durham-Pentz Road (Butte College exit). Turn left onto Durham-Pentz Road, head east 9.2 miles, and turn left on Pentz Road. Drive north 4.4 miles and turn right at the gravel entrance road to Kunkle

Upper Miocene Canal

TO
MAGALIA

Feather
River
Place

22

N

0   0.5   1

MILES

Pentz Road

West Branch Feather River

Upper Miocene Canal

Kunkle
Reservoir

22

22

P → Dam

TO 70

Reservoir. Go another 50 yards and park in the gravel area to the right. There are no restrooms available on this ride.

The Ride

0.0 From the parking area, pedal east past the metal gate, across the earthen dam on a gravel road.

0.2 Turn left onto short gravel area. Go up 30 feet, then right onto singletrack just before Upper Miocene Canal. This dirt trail varies in width from singletrack to doubletrack, running along the south side of the canal.

0.8 The trail becomes narrow with a steep shoulder to the right. Stop and enjoy a good view down into the canyon incised by the Feather River West Branch.

0.9 This is the first of many flume walkways. Any rider turned off by this type of potential hazard should turn around and try another ride.

1.0 CAUTION: Trail is out-sloped.

1.3 Long metal flume walkway.

1.7 70-foot wooden flume walkway.

1.8 Two more wooden flume walkways.

1.9 Short section of narrow trail with a steep shoulder.

2.0 30-foot wooden flume walkway.

2.8 Out-sloped narrow trail.

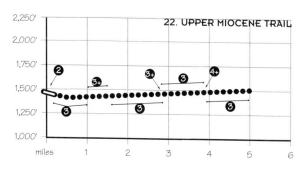

2.9 Walk your bike across wooden ramps.

3.0 50-foot wooden flume crossing, followed by a long (about 150 yards) metal flume walkway.

3.4 Another long metal flume walkway with a nice view of the river and canyon.

3.8 40-foot wooden flume.

3.9 Short rocky section (4+), followed by two successive 40-foot wooden flume walkways.

4.5 Two short wooden ramps.

4.8 60-foot wooden flume walkway followed by a 40-foot wooden flume walkway. Narrow section ahead.

4.9 40-foot wooden flume walkway.

5.0 The metal walkway to the left of the trail allows for passage to the west side of the canal. Turn around here and retrace your route, or try the variation below.

10.1 Back to Kunkle Reservoir parking area.

Variation:

5.0 Cross the flume and begin a strenuous climb up an unimproved road. Go up 50 yards and take a hard left turn, then bear left at a Y junction.

5.9 Go right at a Y.

6.2 Go past a metal road gate and turn left on pavement. Go just 30 feet and turn right on Feather River Place.

6.4 Turn left on Pentz Road.

8.9 Turn left onto the Kunkle Reservoir gravel entrance road. Pedal down 50 yards to your parked vehicle.

Sawmill Peak Lookout

Location: Just east of Magalia, 17 miles northeast of Chico.

Distance: 13.1 miles out and back.

Time: 2 hours.

Tread: 13.1 miles on dirt and gravel roads.

Aerobic level: Strenuous but short.

Technical difficulty: Basic ability to handle dirt roads and fast descents (2+).

Hazards: Excessive speeds on descents are easily attained, owing to steep gradients.

Highlights: Sawmill Peak lookout provides excellent sunset views. This ride is good for a short, intense workout and some fun downhill flying.

Land status: Public roads, Plumas National Forest (lookout area).

Maps: USGS 7.5-minute quad for Paradise East; Plumas National Forest map.

Access: From California Highway 32 and CA 99 in Chico, drive 1.4 miles south on CA 99 and take the Skyway (Paradise/Park Avenue) Exit. Turn left at the end of the off-ramp, heading east toward Paradise. Go 16.9 miles on Skyway and turn right on Coutolenc Road. Park in the little dirt parking area to the right at the intersection of Skyway and Coutolenc Road. (This spot is at the edge of the little town of Magalia.)

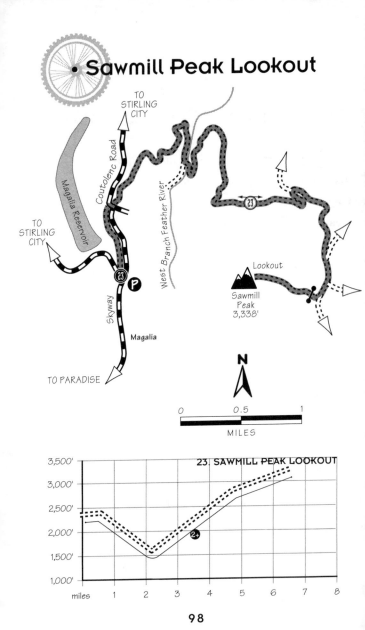

Sawmill Peak Lookout

TO
STIRLING
CITY

Coutolenc Road

Magalia Reservoir

TO
STIRLING
CITY

West Branch Feather River

23

P

Skyway

Magalia

TO PARADISE

N

Lookout

Sawmill
Peak
3,338'

0   0.5   1
MILES

23. SAWMILL PEAK LOOKOUT

3,500'

3,000'

2,500'

2,000'

1,500'

1,000'

2+

miles   1   2   3   4   5   6   7   8

The Ride

0.0 The ride begins on a trail on the north side of Coutolenc Road just across the street from the parking area. Climb up the short, steep embankment heading north. The trail levels off and parallels Coutolenc Road.

0.6 Turn right onto paved Coutolenc Road. Within 50 feet, turn left onto a gravel and dirt road. Stay on your brakes—you'll be dropping 800 feet in less than a mile!

2.1 Turn left onto a bridge across the Feather River West Branch. Commence climbing.

3.7 Keep left. (Serpentine outcropping provides vista point to the right.)

4.7 Take a switchback to the right.

5.6 Turn right at an intersection.

5.8 Go right at a Y junction.

5.9 Go right at another Y, heading west-northwest.

6.3 Go past a yellow steel gate.

6.5 Sawmill Peak fire lookout. Climb up and take in a panoramic view: Bald Mountain to the north; downtown Sacramento to the south; Magalia reservoir, Feather River West Branch, and the Coastal Range to the west. Reverse the route to return to the trailhead. Please keep in mind occasional oncoming cars and trucks as you begin your monomaniacal descent.

13.1 Back at your car.

Old Southern Pacific Grade to Stirling City

Location: On the old railroad grade between Magalia and Stirling City, 17 miles northeast of Chico.

Distance: 25.3 miles out and back.

Time: 2.5 hours.

Tread: 1 mile on paved road; 24.3 miles on unimproved road.

Aerobic level: Moderate.

Technical difficulty: Mostly 2, with one short section of 3+ singletrack, and occasional berms and other barriers installed to exclude four-wheel-drive vehicles (2+ to 3+).

Hazards: Watch for automobile traffic where path crosses paved roads. Trail is partially washed-out at 2.6 miles. Deep ravine at middle of ride (at 5.6 miles) must be circumvented.

Highlights: This ride is a fairly well-maintained dirt road that has replaced an old set of Southern Pacific railroad tracks and is available throughout the year.

Land status: Private land.

Maps: USGS 7.5-minute quads for Paradise East, Stirling City; USGS Chico 1:100,000 map.

Access: From California Highway 32 and CA 99 in Chico, drive 1.4 miles south on CA 99 and take the Skyway (Paradise/Park Avenue) Exit. Turn left at the end of the off-ramp, heading east toward Paradise. Go 16.9 miles on Skyway and turn

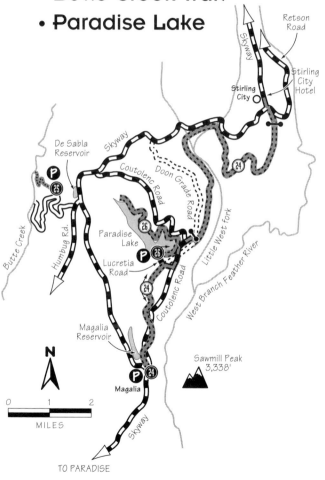

• Old Southern Pacific Grade to Stirling City
• Butte Creek Trail
• Paradise Lake

Retson Road

Skyway

Stirling City

Stirling City Hotel

De Sabla Reservoir

Skyway

Coutolenc Road

Doon Grade Road

(24)

Little West Fork

Butte Creek

Humbug Rd.

Paradise Lake

(26)

Coutolenc Road

West Branch Feather River

Lucretia Road

(24)

Magalia Reservoir

Sawmill Peak 3,338'

Magalia

(24)

N

0   1   2
MILES

Skyway

TO PARADISE

right on Coutolenc Road. Park in the dirt parking area to the right at the intersection of Skyway and Coutolenc Road. (This spot is at the edge of the little town of Magalia.)

The Ride

0.0 The trail begins on the north side of Coutolenc Road just across the street from the parking area. Don't let this steep, rocky start intimidate you—the ride is essentially an old railroad right-of-way with a less than 7 percent grade and fairly smooth going.

0.6 Cross a paved road. Watch out for traffic!

1.1 Stay to the left at fork in the road. Another 75 yards or so and you'll cross another paved road with fast (!) traffic.

2.6 Short section of road has fallen into drainage; keep right!

2.8 Turn right onto a paved road. (This road is Lucretia, but has no sign at this point.)

3.1 Turn left on Coutolenc Road. Yes, this is the same paved road that you left your car parked next to—this smooth, curvy road makes for a beautiful road bike ride to Stirling City.

3.8 Turn right onto Doon Grade Road. Continue up about 75 yards on this dirt road to a green steel gate. This gate was installed presumably to keep low-lifes from using this area as a dump. Take a right here, past the big green gate

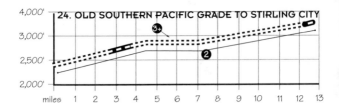

and all the gunshot debris to continue on this otherwise scenic ride.

5.6 The road ends abruptly at a deep ravine! Look up to your left to spot the singletrack detour around the ravine. The singletrack climbs quickly for about 50 feet, then makes a sharp right. In another 50 feet take the lower, right-hand branch at a Y junction and follow this through the drainage and back onto the dirt road.

8.1 Keep left at this branch.

12.5 Pass through a yellow gate, go another 200 yards, and turn left onto paved Retson Road. In 20 yards this road meets Skyway Boulevard. Welcome to Stirling City!

12.7 The large white building on the west side of Skyway just north of Retson is the Stirling City Hotel, the turnaround point for this ride. You can buy anything from a candy bar to a gourmet dinner here. Head back and relax on a long, steady descent to Magalia.

25.3 Back to the beginning.

see map page 101

Butte Creek Trail

Location: Near De Sabla Reservoir, 25 miles northeast of Chico.

Distance: 2.9 miles out and back.

Time: 1 hour.

Tread: 2.9 miles on singletrack.

Aerobic level: Strenuous. Yes, it's less than 3 miles and strenuous.

Technical difficulty: Ride ranges from 3+ to 5+, averaging 4+.

Hazards: The Butte Creek Trail is really a hiking trail. Challenges include impossibly tight switchbacks, steep sections of loose cobbles, and large fixed rocks. Trail is somewhat overgrown with scrub oak and poison oak in spots.

Highlights: A formidable ride to test the strength and balance of any rider. Turnaround point located at a secluded section of Butte Creek in rugged country.

Land status: Owned by Energy Group Project 1; trail open to the public.

Maps: USGS 7.5-minute quads for Paradise East, Paradise West, and Cohasset. (That's right—1.5 miles of trail happens to fall on the corners of three maps!)

Access: From California Highway 32 and CA 99 in Chico, drive 1.4 miles south on CA 99 and take the Skyway (Paradise/Park Avenue) Exit. Turn left at the end of the off-ramp, heading east toward Paradise. Drive 22.2 miles, through Paradise Pines, and turn left onto Humbug Road (at the PG & E maintenance yard). Go up 0.3 mile and turn right onto a gravel road

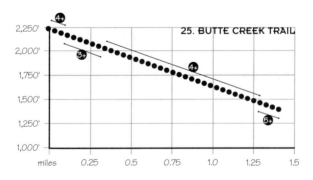

without any street signage. Notice the large white sign 50 yards ahead on the right side of the road; this gives directions to Butte Creek Trail, and a detailed map of the area. Continue down the gravel road 1.5 miles and turn right at a hairpin turn in the road. Drive to the end of this cul-de-sac (about 0.1 mile) and park.

The Ride

0.0 Start pedaling onto singletrack from the west end of the parking area. The singletrack starts out rocky and steep (4+).

0.1 Singletrack merges onto a wider trail 30 feet before a wooden bulletin board/kiosk. Remember this juncture for your return. Ride down past the kiosk and settle in to some easier going (3+).

0.3 At a small gully, take singletrack to the right, heading southwest, rather than the wider trail to the left.

0.7 Watch out for an abrupt switchback to the left; the trail's edge drops off sharply.

1.3 The trail begins to drop steeply, with impossibly tight switchbacks (5+).

1.4 The trail ends at Butte Creek. A small swimming hole lies about 50 feet upstream. Retrace your route to return to the trailhead. The climb out is strenuous.

2.8 Remember to turn right 30 feet after the wooden kiosk.

2.9 Back to the parking area.

see map page 101

Paradise Lake

Location: 22 miles northeast of Chico.

Distance: 9.3 miles out and back.

Time: 1 hour.

Tread: 9.3 miles on unimproved dirt road (which has been converted to a hiking/biking path).

Aerobic level: Easy.

Technical difficulty: Mostly 2 with a few ruts and vines (2+).

Hazards: This ride is fairly benign, but use caution when approaching occasional ruts and thorny vines. Paradise Lake is closed on Wednesdays.

Highlights: This peaceful, easy ride along the shore is well shaded by a variety of trees, and is fairly close to Chico.

Land status: Paradise Irrigation District.

Maps: USGS 7.5-minute quad for Paradise East.

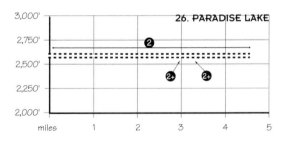

Access: From California Highway 32 and CA 99 in Chico, drive 1.4 miles south on CA 99 and take the Skyway (Paradise/ Park Avenue) Exit. Turn left at the end of the off-ramp, heading east toward Paradise. Go 16.9 miles on Skyway and turn right on Coutolenc Road. Drive 2.8 miles and turn left on Lucretia. Continue 0.6 mile to the Paradise Lake entrance; go up 100 feet and turn left, toward the fishing area parking. Drive down 100 yards and park in parking area.

The Ride

0.0 From the end of the parking lot (by the portable toilets), turn right onto the dirt path near the shore, heading east.
0.7 Stay on the wide path, bearing left.
1.6 Stream crossing.
2.1 Cut across a gravel road near the water's edge.
2.7 Go around a green steel gate; stay left, near the shore. Cycle up another 50 yards and around another gate.
3.0 Slightly rocky ahead (2+).
3.3 Bear left where another road ties into this one. Go past another green steel gate.
3.4 Rocks and vines ahead (2+).
4.3 Stream crossing.
4.5 Another small stream.
4.6 End of the road. Turn around here and return to your car.
9.3 Back to parking area.

POA West

Location: Paradise Pines, 23 miles northeast of Chico.

Distance: 5.4 miles out and back

Time: 30 minutes to 1 hour.

Tread: 5.4 miles of well-maintained singletrack.

Aerobic level: Easy to moderate, depending on pace.

Technical difficulty: Averages about 3+; several technical sections can be walked.

Hazards: Loose soil and forest litter provide poor traction in some sections; occasional poison oak; overhanging branches at eye level; two short, very steep sections that should be walked both for safety's sake and to prevent erosion.

Highlights: Very pretty riparian setting; entirely shaded by a thick forest; well-maintained singletrack; close to town. This great singletrack is on private land. Please be considerate of hikers and mindful of the erosive effects of skidding on trails.

Land status: Paradise Pines Property Owners Association (POA).

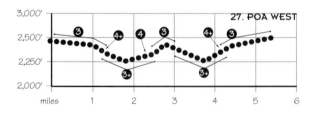

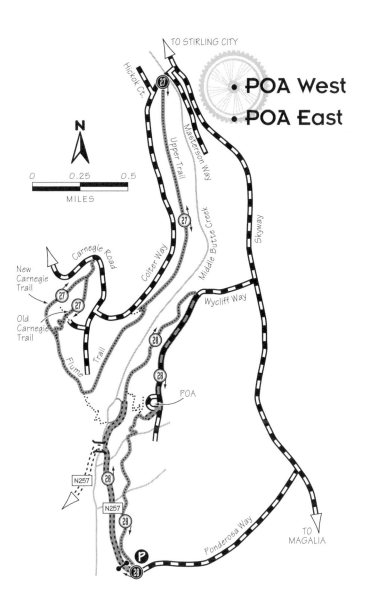

TO STIRLING CITY

POA West
POA East

Hickok Ck.

27

Masterson Way

Upper Trail

N

0   0.25   0.5
MILES

Skyway

27

Middle Butte Creek

Carnegie Road

New Carnegie Trail

27

Colter Way

Wycliff Way

Old Carnegie Trail

27

28

Flume Trail

28

POA

28

N257

28

N257

28

Ponderosa Way

P

28

TO MAGALIA

109

Maps: USGS 7.5-minute quad for Paradise East.

Access: From California Highway 32 and CA 99 in Chico, drive 1.4 miles south on CA 99 and take the Skyway (Paradise/Park Avenue) Exit. Turn left at the end of the off-ramp, heading east toward Paradise. Go 20.6 miles on Skyway and turn left on Colter Way. Find a wide shoulder and park. The ride starts at a singletrack trailhead on the south side of Colter Way, between Masterson Way and Hickok Court.

The Ride

0.0 Carefully walk down the first 30 feet of trail and begin pedaling south on singletrack along a fence.

0.9 Go left at a Y junction.

1.2 Five-way intersection. Take a hard left (at tire steps), heading northeast. Sign on the right reads "Colter Exit #6 Colter/Masterson." The trail descends steeply through a couple of switchbacks, and then becomes too steep to ride without skidding tires. Please dismount and walk your bike down this short section.

1.7 Bear right at a T junction; pass by a branch to the Lower Trail—Ponderosa/POA.

2.0 Pass by old sections of flume pipes.

2.2 Bear left, staying on Flume Trail; go past a branch to Wayne Court. Pass through a small rocky gully.

2.3 Walk across another gully, where three trails branch off. Take the far left branch, heading north, alongside an intermittent stream ravine.

2.5 Turn left onto a wide trail.

2.6 Stay left.

2.7 Turn around at paved Carnegie Road, and head back down the singletrack.

2.9 Stay left here, toward the Flume Trail, passing by the branch to the right on which you came up.

3.1   Go straight through an intersection, heading south.

3.2   Turn left onto Flume Trail. From this point on, retrace your route back to your automobile.

4.1   Keep left at a Y; continue and turn left at another Y, up a steep climb.

4.2   Turn right on Upper Trail.

5.4   Back to the beginning.

see map page 109

POA East

Location: Paradise Pines, 21 miles northeast of Chico.

Distance: 3.5-mile loop.

Time: 30 minutes to 1 hour.

Tread: 0.6 mile on paved road; 1.1 miles on unimproved road; 1.8 miles on singletrack.

Aerobic level: Moderate, with 0.4 mile of strenuous climbing. (Reverse the route for an easier loop.)

Technical difficulty: Averages about 3, with nothing more difficult than 4.

Hazards: Poison oak; sections of narrow singletrack with soft shoulders and loose forest litter.

Highlights: A fast, fun loop; beautiful singletrack along Butte Creek; close to Chico.

Land status: Paradise Pines Property Owners Association (POA).

Maps: USGS 7.5-minute quad for Paradise East.

Access: From California Highway 32 and CA 99 in Chico, drive 1.4 miles south on CA 99 and take the Skyway (Paradise/Park Avenue) Exit. Turn left at the end of the off-ramp, heading east toward Paradise. Go 18.2 miles on Skyway and turn left on Ponderosa Way. In 1 mile Ponderosa Way becomes unimproved (County Road N257). Continue another 0.1 mile on this unpaved portion of Ponderosa Way and turn right at a Y junction; park in the dirt clearing.

The Ride

0.0 From the dirt parking area pedal down Ponderosa Way (County Road N257). Head northwest and ride around a yellow steel road gate. A fast descent ahead includes large fixed rocks, ruts, and loose gravel and cobbles.

0.6 Pass a waterfall on the right.

0.8 Turn right onto a rough jeep trail, just before Ponderosa Way (CR N257) crosses Butte Creek.

1.0 The trail runs alongside Butte Creek and narrows to singletrack.

1.1 Bear right, passing C-Nic trail.

1.2 Go right at a Y.

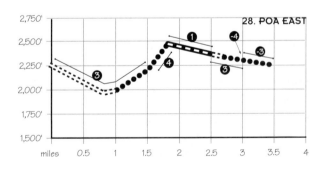

- **1.3** Cross an intermittent stream.
- **1.4** Begin a tough climb. The steep grade and loose surface may require walking.
- **1.8** Turn right on paved Wycliff Way and catch your breath!
- **2.4** Turn right into POA entrance (50 yards past POA exit); go another 50 yards and turn off the entrance road on the left side, just before "Horseshoe Pit" sign.
- **2.5** Pick up doubletrack on the left side of the entrance road; head south; go up another 70 yards and turn left at a Y.
- **2.6** The trail narrows to singletrack.
- **2.7** Make a hard left at a Y, toward Ponderosa Way. (Notice the sign at this junction.) After a couple of turns, the trail crosses a stream.
- **3.0** CAUTION: short descent with ruts ahead (-4).
- **3.5** Back to Ponderosa Way parking area.

Doe Mill Ridge

Location: Just east of Chico, starting on the eastern edge of town.

Distance: 28.6-mile loop.

Time: 3 hours.

Tread: 19.6 miles on paved road; 1.1 miles on gravel road; 7.9 miles on unimproved road.

Aerobic level: Mostly moderate, with about 3 miles of strenuous climbing.

Technical difficulty: 1 on pavement; 2 to 4 on unimproved road.

Hazards: Bruce Road has narrow shoulders and fast automobile traffic; watch for a surprising turn at about 17.3 miles.

Highlights: Verdant riparian corridor along Butte Creek from Skyway Boulevard to Center Gap Road is lush with vegetation year-round.

Land status: City of Chico; Butte County; 9 miles of private road.

Maps: USGS 7.5-minute quads for Chico, Hamlin Canyon, Paradise West; local street maps (for example, Rand McNally—Butte County).

Access: From California Highway 32 and CA 99 in Chico, go 1.5 miles east on CA 32. Turn right on Bruce Road and drive south 0.4 mile to the intersection of Humboldt Road and Bruce Road. Find a wide shoulder and park.

The Ride

0.0   Pedal south on Bruce Road. Keep right because traffic can be slightly menacing on Bruce Road. (Wear brightly colored clothing for this ride.)

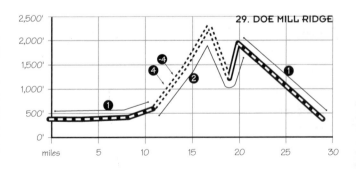

Doe Mill Ridge

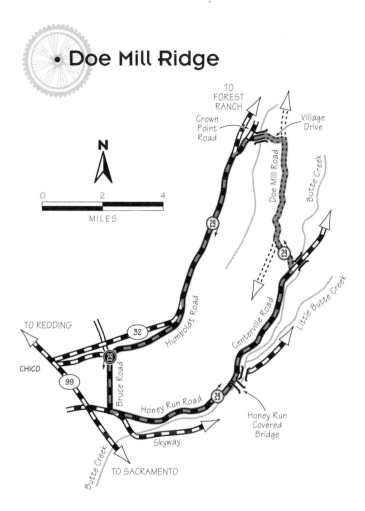

TO
FOREST
RANCH

Crown
Point
Road

Village
Drive

Doe Mill Road

Butte Creek

29

29

N

0   2   4

MILES

Centerville Road

Little Butte Creek

TO REDDING

32

Humboldt Road

CHICO

29

99

Bruce Road

Honey Run Road

29

Honey Run
Covered
Bridge

Butte Creek

Skyway

TO SACRAMENTO

1.6 Turn left on Skyway Boulevard and travel east-southeast 0.6 mile. Skyway bisects a small wetland area here— watch for hunting kites and hawks.

2.4 Turn left on Honey Run Road. (A driving range is on the right and Kingdom Hall is on the left.) Ride northeast on Honey Run Road alongside Butte Creek for about 4.5 miles. Traffic is sparse except on weekends and during commute hours.

6.8 Honey Run Covered Bridge, built in 1896. Here's a great place to stop and enjoy Butte Creek. Telephone, restrooms, and drinking water are available here. Continue on Honey Run Road another 30 yards or so and turn left on Centerville Road—formerly named Humbug Road. (Roadies will enjoy climbing 5.5 miles on Honey Run Road up to Paradise.) Pedal north-northeast on Centerville Road, continuing alongside Butte Creek for another 3.6 miles.

10.5 Turn left on Center Gap Road. You are finally on the dirt; here's where the fun begins! Now is a good time to lower your tire pressure and catch your breath. Plan on climbing 1,000 feet in 2 miles.

10.7 Stay to the right to remain on Center Gap Road.

11.9 The road gets steeper (strenuous) and is washed out, with loose pebbles and cobbles (4). Stay to the left when you see the off-camber rock and you can make this section cleanly.

12.4 Gradient eases and the road is smoother.

12.6 Center Gap Road ends at Doe Mill Road. Ride straight ahead to the north. Vegetation is mostly chaparral for the next few miles.

13.1 Steeper and more technical (-4) for about 0.3 mile.

15.2 Back among the trees—digger pine and scrub oak.

16.0 Turn left onto Village Drive, heading west.

16.5 At an elevation of 2,230 feet, this is the apex of the ride. Enjoy moderate acceleration for the next 0.4 mile.

16.9 More fun—don't let it go to your head as you swoop into this radical, curvy, 2-mile descent.

17.3 An unexpected (!) tight left turn at a T in the road.

18.4 A wooden bridge takes you across Little Chico Creek, elevation 1,200 feet. The road is smooth, well-maintained gravel. Expect to climb 700 feet in the next mile!

19.5 Turn left onto pavement at Crown Point Road.

19.7 Turn left onto CA 32, heading south back to Chico. Please be mindful of 60 miles-per-hour traffic. It's all downhill from here!

25.0 Turn left onto Humboldt Road. Relax and enjoy the scenery.

28.6 Back to Bruce Road and your automobile.

Garland Road

Location: 18 miles northeast of Chico, just past Forest Ranch.

Distance: 11 miles out and back.

Time: 1.5 to 2 hours.

Tread: 0.2 mile on paved road; 8.8 miles on unimproved road; 2 miles on singletrack.

Aerobic level: Mostly easy with a moderate climb at the end.

Technical difficulty: Averages about 2+.

Hazards: Fairly high speeds can easily be reached descending Doe Mill Road, which is loose, bumpy, and rocky. Some poison oak on singletrack.

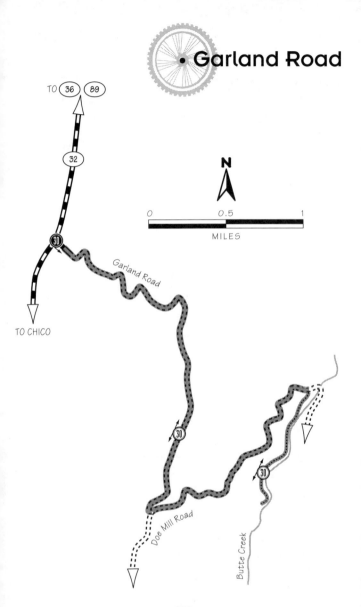

Garland Road

TO 36 89

32

30

TO CHICO

N

0   0.5   1

MILES

Garland Road

30

30

Doe Mill Road

Butte Creek

Highlights: For a quick, fun workout fairly close to Chico, try this ride. It includes some exciting downhill on dirt roads, as well as some very pretty countryside, especially along the singletrack overlooking Butte Creek.

Land status: U.S. Bureau of Land Management.

Maps: USGS 7.5-minute quads for Cohasset, Stirling City.

Access: From California Highway 32 and CA 99 in Chico, drive 18.2 miles northeast on CA 32 and park on the highway shoulder at Garland Road.

The Ride

0.0   Pedal southeast down Garland Road.
0.1   Garland Road changes from paved to unimproved.
1.2   The road begins to descend more quickly. Watch out for large fixed rocks.
2.6   Turn left onto Doe Mill Road.
4.5   Make a hard right onto singletrack, about 50 yards before Doe Mill Road crosses Butte Creek.
4.7   Cross over a gully on a wooden footbridge.
4.8   Another wooden footbridge.
4.9   Cross another short footbridge. In about 100 yards, cross a gravel road and continue on singletrack.

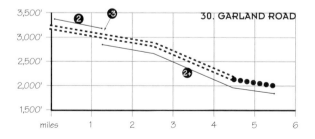

5.0 Notice where Butte Creek has cut sharply into the green serpentine rock and polished it nicely.

5.2 Climb up a set of rickety wooden stairs—carefully! Pedal another 50 yards, then climb down a shorter set of wooden stairs.

5.4 Trail is partially washed out here. Carefully climb through this short section and continue another 50 yards for a view of some deep pools and the turnaround point.

5.5 Take in a good view, then turn around and retrace your route.

6.5 Back on Doe Mill Road; pay for that fun descent!

11.0 Back to your car.

Appendix A

Information Sources

Chico Velo Cycling Club
P.O. Box 2285
Chico, CA 95927
800-482-2453

City of Chico Parks Department
411 Main Street
Chico, CA 95928
530-895-4972

City of Oroville
1735 Montgomery Street
Oroville, CA 95965
530-538-2401

Plumas National Forest
Feather River Ranger District
875 Mitchell Avenue
Oroville, CA 95965
530-534-6500

Tahoe National Forest
North Yuba Ranger Station
15924 Highway 49
Camptonville, CA 95922-9707
530-288-3231

Lassen National Forest
Almanor Ranger District
P.O. Box 767
Chester, CA 96020
530-258-2141

United States Bureau of Land Management
Redding Resource Area Office
355 Hemstead Drive
Redding, CA 96002-0910
530-224-2100

Appendix B

Bike Shops

Bike Barn
845 Main Street
Chico, CA 95928
530-343-5506

Bike Lane
346 Broadway
Chico, CA 95928
530-345-2453

Campus Bicycles
330 Main Street
Chico, CA 95928
530-345-2081

Chico Bicycle
127 Main Street
Chico, CA 95928
530-345-2613

Chico Sports Ltd.
240 Main St.
Chico, CA 95928
530-894-1110

Cycle Sport
222 West 2nd Street
Chico, CA 95928
530-345-1910

Family Cyclery
260 East 1st Street
Chico, CA 95928
530-893-8362

Greenline Cycles
1117 Oro Dam Boulevard
Oroville, CA 95965
530-533-7885

North Valley Bicycle
2590 Cohasset Road
Chico, CA 95973
530-343-0636

Pullins Cyclery
801 Main Street
Chico, CA 95928
530-342-1055

Village Cycle
1311 Mangrove Avenue
Chico, CA 95926
530-342-2431

Glossary

ATB: All-terrain bicycle; a.k.a. mountain bike, sprocket rocket, fat tire flyer.

ATV: All-terrain vehicle; in this book ATV refers to motorbikes and three- and four-wheelers designed for off-road use.

Bail: Getting off the bike, usually in a hurry, and whether or not you meant to. Often a last resort.

Bunny hop: Leaping up, while riding, and lifting both wheels off the ground to jump over an obstacle (or for sheer joy).

Clamper cramps: That burning, cramping sensation experienced in the hands during extended braking.

Clean: To ride without touching a foot (or other body part) to the ground; to ride a tough section successfully.

Clipless: A type of pedal with a binding that accepts a special cleat on the soles of bike shoes. The cleat clicks in for more control and efficient pedaling and out for safe landings (in theory).

Contour: A line on a topographic map showing a continuous elevation level over uneven ground. Also used as a verb to indicate a fairly easy or moderate grade: "The trail contours around the canyon rim before the final grunt to the top."

Dab: To put a foot or hand down (or hold onto or lean on a tree or other support) while riding. If you have to dab, then you haven't ridden that piece of trail **clean**.

Downfall: Trees that have fallen across the trail.

Doubletrack: A trail, jeep road, ATV route, or other track with two distinct ribbons of **tread**, typically with grass growing in between. No matter which side you choose, the other rut always looks smoother.

Endo: Lifting the rear wheel off the ground and riding (or abruptly not riding) on the front wheel only. Also known, at various degrees of control and finality, as a nose wheelie, "going over the handlebars," and a face plant.

Fall line: The angle and direction of a slope; the **line** you follow when gravity is in control and you aren't.

Graded: When a gravel road is scraped level to smooth out the washboards and potholes, it has been graded. In this book, a road is listed as graded only if it is regularly maintained. Not all such roads are graded every year, however.

Granny gear: The lowest (easiest) gear, a combination of the smallest of the three chainrings on the bottom bracket spindle (where the pedals and crank arms attach to the bike's frame) and the largest cog on the rear cluster. Shift down to your granny gear for serious climbing.

Hammer: To ride hard; derived from how it feels afterward: "I'm hammered."

Hammerhead: Someone who actually enjoys feeling **hammered**. A Type-A personality rider who goes hard and fast all the time.

Kelly hump: An abrupt mound of dirt across the road or trail. These are common on old logging roads and skidder tracks, placed there to block vehicle access. At high speeds, they become launching pads for bikes and inadvertent astronauts.

Line: The route (or trajectory) between or over obstacles or through turns. **Tread** or trail refers to the ground you're riding on; the line is the path you choose within the tread (and exists mostly in the eye of the beholder).

Off-the-seat: Moving your butt behind the bike seat and over the rear tire; used for control on extremely steep descents. This position increases braking power, helps prevent **endos**, and reduces skidding.

Portage: To carry the bike, usually up a steep hill, across unrideable obstacles, or through a stream.

Quads: Thigh muscles (short for quadriceps) or maps in the USGS topographic series (short for quadrangles). Nice quads of either kind can help get you out of trouble in the backcountry.

Ratcheting: Also known as backpedaling; pedaling backward to avoid hitting rocks or other obstacles with the pedals.

Sidehill: Where the trail crosses a slope. If the **tread** is narrow, keep your inside (uphill) pedal up to avoid hitting the ground. If the tread tilts downhill, you may have to use some body language to keep the bike plumb or vertical to avoid slipping out.

Singletrack: A trail, game run, or other track with only one ribbon of **tread**. But this is like defining an orgasm as a muscle cramp. Good singletrack is pure fun.

Spur: A side road or trail that splits off from the main route.

Surf: Riding through loose gravel or sand, when the wheels sway from side to side. Also *heavy surf*: frequent and difficult obstacles.

Suspension: A bike with front suspension has a shock-absorbing fork or stem. Rear suspension absorbs shock between the rear wheel and frame. A bike with both is said to be fully suspended.

Switchbacks: When a trail goes up a steep slope, it zigzags or *switchbacks* across the fall line to ease the gradient of the climb. Well-designed switchbacks make a turn with at least an 8-foot radius and remain fairly level within the turn itself. These are rare, however, and cyclists often struggle to ride through sharply angled, sloping switchbacks.

Track stand: Balancing on a bike in one place, without rolling forward appreciably. Cock the front wheel to one side and bring that pedal up to the one or two o'clock position. Now control your side-to-side balance by applying pressure on the pedals and brakes and changing the angle of the front wheel, as needed. It takes practice but really comes in handy at stoplights, on **switchbacks**, and when trying to free a foot before falling.

Tread: The riding surface, particularly regarding **singletrack**.

Water bar: A log, rock, or other barrier placed in the **tread** to divert water off the trail and prevent erosion. Peeled logs can be slippery and cause bad falls, especially when they angle sharply across the trail.

Whoop-dee-doo: A series of kelly humps used to keep vehicles off trails. Watch your speed or do the dreaded top tube tango.

Appendix C

A Short Index of Rides

Road Rides
(includes jeep tracks and unmaintained routes)
1. Lower Bidwell Park
2. Upper Park Road
7. Ten Mile House Road
9. Upper Ponderosa Way
11. Colby Mountain Lookout
12. Humbug Summit
13. Humboldt Summit
14. Philbrook Lake to Lotts Lake
21. Camp Creek Road
23. Sawmill Peak Lookout
24. Old Southern Pacific Grade to Stirling City
26. Paradise Lake
29. Doe Mill Ridge
30. Garland Road

Sweet Singletrack Rides
(may also include road and doubletrack portions)
3. Lower Trail
4. Middle Trail
5. North Rim Trail
6. South Rim Trail
8. Pine Trail
10. Deer Creek Trail
16. (West) Bullards Bar Trail
17. (East) Bullards Bar Trail
18. Eight Ball Trail

FALCON GUIDES Leading the Way™

FALCON GUIDES are available for where-to-go hiking, mountain biking, rock climbing, walking, scenic driving, fishing, rockhounding, paddling, birding, wildlife viewing, and camping. We also have FalconGuides on essential outdoor skills and subjects and field identification. The following titles are currently available, but this list grows every year. For a free catalog with a complete list of titles, call FALCON toll-free at 1-800-582-2665.

MOUNTAIN BIKING

Mountain Biking Arizona
Mountain Biking Colorado
Mountain Biking Georgia
Mountain Biking New Mexico
Mountain Biking New York
Mountain Biking Northern
 New England
Mountain Biking Oregon
Mountain Biking South Carolina
Mountain Biking Southern California
Mountain Biking Southern
 New England
Mountain Biking Utah
Mountain Biking Wisconsin
Mountain Biking Wyoming

LOCAL CYCLING SERIES

Fat Trax Bozeman
Mountain Biking Bend
Mountain Biking Boise
Mountain Biking Chequamegon
Mountain Biking Chico
Mountain Biking Colorado Springs
Mountain Biking Denver/Boulder
Mountain Biking Durango
Mountain Biking Flagstaff and
 Sedona
Mountain Biking Helena
Mountain Biking Moab
Mountain Biking White Mountains
Mountain Biking Utah's St. George/
 Cedar City Area

■ *To order any of these books, check with your local*
bookseller or call FALCON ® at
1-800-582-2665*.*
www.FalconOutdoors.com

FALCON®

FALCON GUIDES® Leading the Way™

SCENIC DRIVING GUIDES

Scenic Driving Alaska and the Yukon
Scenic Driving Arizona
Scenic Driving the Beartooth Highway
Scenic Driving California
Scenic Driving Colorado
Scenic Driving Florida
Scenic Driving Georgia
Scenic Driving Hawaii
Scenic Driving Idaho
Scenic Driving Michigan
Scenic Driving Minnesota
Scenic Driving Montana
Scenic Driving New England
Scenic Driving New Mexico
Scenic Driving North Carolina
Scenic Driving Oregon
Scenic Driving the Ozarks
Scenic Driving Pennsylvania
Scenic Driving Texas
Scenic Driving Utah
Scenic Driving Washington
Scenic Driving Wisconsin
Scenic Driving Wyoming
Scenic Driving Yellowstone and Grand
   Teton National Parks
Scenic Byways East
Scenic Byways Far West
Scenic Byways Rocky Mountains
Back Country Byways
Traveling California's Gold Rush Country
Traveling the Lewis & Clark Trail
Traveling the Oregon Trail
Traveler's Guide to the Pony Express Trail

WILDLIFE VIEWING GUIDES

Alaska Wildlife Viewing Guide
Arizona Wildlife Viewing Guide
California Wildlife Viewing Guide
Colorado Wildlife Viewing Guide
Florida Wildlife Viewing Guide
Indiana Wildlife Veing Guide
Iowa Wildlife Viewing Guide
Kentucky Wildlife Viewing Guide
Massachusetts Wildlife Viewing Guide
Montana Wildlife Viewing Guide
Nebraska Wildlife Viewing Guide
Nevada Wildlife Viewing Guide
New Hampshire Wildlife Viewing Guide
New Jersey Wildlife Viewing Guide
New Mexico Wildlife Viewing Guide
New York Wildlife Viewing Guide
North Carolina Wildlife Viewing Guide
North Dakota Wildlife Viewing Guide
Ohio Wildlife Viewing Guide
Oregon Wildlife Viewing Guide
Puerto Rico & the Virgin Islands
   Wildlife Viewing Guide
Tennessee Wildlife Viewing Guide
Texas Wildlife Viewing Guide
Utah Wildlife Viewing Guide
Vermont Wildlife Viewing Guide
Virginia Wildlife Viewing Guide
Washington Wildlife Viewing Guide
West Virginia Wildife Viewing Guide
Wisconsin Wildlife Viewing Guide

FALCON®